OWN YOUR GREATNESS

A Guide To Creating A Life
With Boundless Possibilities

To Karen,
With much
love.
Nora
Lapitan
11/12/04

Nora Lapitan, Ph.D.

Empowered Living
Fort Collins, Colorado

Published by:
Empowered Living, LLC
1020 Braidwood Ct.
Fort Collins, CO 80524
http://www.Own-Your-Greatness.com

Publisher's Cataloging-in-Publication
(Provided by Quality Books, Inc.)

Lapitan, Nora
   Own Your Greatness : a guide to creating a life with boundless possibilities / Nora Lapitan.
   p. cm
   Includes bibliographical references and index.
   LCCN 2004109625
   ISBN 0-9758374-0
   1. Self-realization. 2. Conduct of life. 3. Interpersonal relations.
4. Self-actualization (Pyschology) I. Title

BF637.S4L36 2004   158.1
                          QB104-800040

Book and Cover Design by Eris Klein

Printed in the United States of America
10 9 8 7 6 5 4 3 2 1

To Daddy
For giving me eyes to see
possibilities in human beings

To Mike
For giving me tools to live
my life out of possibilities

To God
The ultimate source of all possibilities

Whatever we do, we do out of love or
out of fear.

When you allow love to lead the way,
you are living your greatness.

- NL

TABLE OF CONTENTS

ACKNOWLEDGMENTS

W hat has made the publication of this book possible are the people behind its making. I am deeply grateful to the following individuals for their direct support in the preparation of this book and the impact they have had in my life.

To my life partner, Romel, for seeing possibilities in me that I sometimes could not see. For supporting me in this project the whole way, for your patience during those times when I was oblivious to everything else while I was writing, and taking care of the details of publishing. I would not be where I am today if it had not been for your love and unwavering support in the past 23 years of our life together.

To Holley Zadeh-Gardel, Sara Simonson, Mark Alan, Lori Mc-Connaughey, Mike Smith, and Patricia Brown, for your feedback on the drafts of this manuscript. You helped shape the book into what it is. To Cindy Griffin, when I was ready to shelf this project, your encouragement kept me going.

Holley, you are a dear friend. Thank you for listening and giving me space to be human. Everyone needs a friend like you.

To Eris Klein, for the cover art and the internal layout of this book. You made this book more beautiful than I had imagined it to be. Though I have not known you for a long time, I feel deeply connected with you. You have made the final steps of publishing this book so much fun.

To Mike Smith, this book would not be in existence if I had

never met you. Thank you for your commitment to my development. I have been blessed because you expressed your gifts in the world. You inspire me to live my possibilities.

To Tinka Smith, for your commitment to human beings. For being the quiet power that you are. For making the "Freedom Course" possible through the safety that you provide.

To my friends in the "Mastery community", for making me feel heard, which started me on the path of listening to my heart. To friends whose situations I used as examples in this book, thank you for generously sharing your experiences and insights.

To Linda V. Jimeno, you inspire me with how you live your life. You have shown me what it means to live for a purpose greater than yourself. I am proud of you, dear Sister.

Ronnie and Reggie, you are the light of my life. When I watch you guys, you remind me of what is possible for human beings, and of what is truly important in life. What a gift you are to the world!

Finally, to my parents. Although they have passed on, their love continues to live in me.

INTRODUCTION

- Do you drag yourself out of bed in the morning and dread the day ahead of you?

- Have your days become a string of have-to-do's?

- Have you forgotten what it feels like to be excited about what you're doing?

- Are you still wondering what you want to be when you grow up?

- Do you have a dream and are you waiting for the right time to live it? Or have you given up on your dreams?

- Have you ever asked yourself, "Is there more to life than this?"

If you answered yes to any of these questions, read on.

Human beings are magnificent. Each person comes with unique gifts and a way of seeing the world that others would love to have access to. But we are also forgetful. We have forgotten what we love, what we are good at, and what we dream of creating in the world. This book is about reconnecting with our possibilities, discovering once again what we love and care about. This book is about owning our greatness. To **own** something means to acknowledge that it belongs to us. To own our greatness is to also own our weaknesses. Once we can do that, we are free to be ourselves, and to share our gifts with the world.

Do you remember a time when you were young that nothing was too big for you? Children seem to know intuitively what their true nature is. As a little girl, I would look up to the stars and say to myself, "I can reach for the stars, I can make a difference." I was excited about life and believed I could do anything I put my heart on. In the process of growing up I forgot my nature.

Early in my life I watched my father resign to the circumstances of his life. He was a brilliant man whom I adored. An engineer, mathematician, poet, literature lover, he was also a compassionate man who believed in people. I saw him as the embodiment of what was possible for human beings. And yet he had his own problems and he started drinking when he was in his early 40s. I watched as he drank more and more over the years, and toward the end of his life, he spent more hours unconscious than awake. I can think of no sadder thing than for people to die while they are still alive. Norman Cousins (1915-90) said, "Death is not the greatest loss in life. The greatest loss is what dies inside of us while we live."

As I look back to those years, I realize I made a promise to myself that my life would be different. At the age of 25, I left my home country, the Philippines, and came to the United States to pursue a graduate education. I thought I had a formula for success and happiness: get a Ph.D. degree, be a successful scientist, get a good job with a university, have children, keep my marriage. I did it all. One day, I woke up feeling empty and asking myself, "is this all there is to life?" My life had become mere drudgery, going through the motions day after day. I was resigned to the circum-stances of my life. How ironic – what I set out not to become, I became! (Later I learned that this made perfect sense).

I thought I knew the answers to life and the answers failed me. It is said when the student is ready, the teacher appears. It was at this time when I met a man named Mike Smith[1], who developed and led a course called the Freedom Course. I took the course and this was the beginning of my journey to awakening. It was as if I had died and I began to live again. This was the start of my transformation. Mike has become my mentor. He is also a real friend. I have come to realize that a real friend is someone who is so committed to me, he will risk losing my friendship and business if that's what it takes for me to see the truth about myself. Truths that I was not willing to face, although the evidence was all around me.

We are the last to see ourselves. There's a saying, "Air to the bird, water to the fish, and man to himself." Life always hands us our lessons. The problem is, we are blind to them. Deeply embedded in ourselves and our habits, we are blind to who we are being and our role in creating the circumstances of our lives. We keep doing the same things and expect to get different results. One of Mike's contributions to me is his brutal honesty, which he speaks with a lot of love. No matter how difficult, I was willing to look at what he wanted me to see because of that love. That love carried me far. As I think about hundreds of other people who have worked with Mike, I am humbled to realize how one person's love can transform many lives.

I embarked on a research project to answer this question - **how do human beings reconnect with their greatness?** This book is

---

[1] Michael Smith is co-founder of the Center for Leadership Design. Information on the Freedom Course is available at http://www.freedomfoundationinc.com or at 1-888-412-8720.

my attempt to summarize what I learned in my own life and from the lives of friends on the same path, as well as from my readings of books in human psychology and spirituality. This book is heavily influenced by Mike Smith's work, because of the impact he has had in my life. There are also materials taken from the Bible and other spiritual sources. I realize that some people may be turned off by religious content. This book is not about religion, so I am asking that you keep an open mind and see the message that is being offered, regardless of the source.

I learned that transforming our lives to what is possible does not require having more skills, money, or knowledge, although these are helpful to have. What is essential is love. All of us have the capacity to love. When we are in love, we experience joy, contentment, and satisfaction. We feel deeply connected to ourselves, and to those we love. Love can be generated. We can get in touch with feelings of love by doing things that nurture our spirit, such as being in the ocean or mountains, listening to music, reading poetry, or whatever it is that we enjoy doing. My experience of God is presence of love that is boundless in depth and breadth. Different people may have different names for this loving presence, including Universe, Higher Self, etc. If human love can transform lives, our possibilities are limitless in that loving presence. Whatever we do, we do out of love or out of fear. When you allow love to lead the way, you are living your greatness.

I write this book for my father. It is my way of expressing what I wish I spoke to him while he was alive. I also write it for my children, and every child in the world, so they may never forget their greatness when they grow up. Finally, I write it for every person who is ready to get in touch with his or her greatness and share it with the world.

This book is about possibilities and ways of seeing ourselves and the world that empower us. I write from a commitment to share truthfully and generously what I have learned about human tendencies and to show what is possible for human beings. The book is not about getting somewhere. It is not about becoming great in a year or ten years. You already are great. The lessons presented are to empower you to make choices in the present that are in line with your highest nature. It is in the present where your power lives. Jesus Christ said, "Unless you become like children, you cannot enter the kingdom of God."[2] Children live only for the moment. This work is a way of life that brings satisfaction and aliveness today, right here and now.

Are you ready?

The purpose of this book is to give us access to our personal power in creating a life that is an expression of our greatest possibilities. This is accomplished by lessons combined with real examples, and exercises at the end of each chapter.

The book is divided into three parts. In Part I, we will look at our reality and circumstances, and our own role in creating what we have in our lives. Looking at ourselves honestly can be difficult, especially when we begin to realize our role in creating those things we do not want. When you are tempted to stop, just notice and

---

[2] Matthew 19: 13.

know that this is a natural reaction. Before we can create something new, something that we really want, it is important that we first understand our role in creating what we have. In Part II, we will look at creating new possibilities, creating a future that is in line with our greatest vision for ourselves. Part III takes us beyond making our own lives work to one of making our lives an instrument of service for others and leaving a legacy in the world.

The lessons presented in this book are not THE truth. They are ways of seeing our circumstances in a different light and being open to other possibilities. The best way to get the most out of this book is to be actively engaged. This book will only be as useful to the degree that you are willing to be engaged. Rather than take a lesson at face value, test it in your own life and see what results you get. If it works, keep it. If not, throw it out. The ultimate test is whether it works for you. A caveat: these lessons are not quick-fix solutions to your problems. Although you can expect to see immediate results in the quality of your experiences, changes in the physical realm may take time. Be patient with yourself. Take notice of your progress. Growth and transformation are life-long processes.

Questions and exercises at the end of each chapter provide an opportunity to test the lessons in your life. Questions are powerful tools for learning. When you ask a question, you begin noticing things that you did not see before. Sometimes what you discover may make you feel uncomfortable or even ashamed. Give yourself permission to be honest with yourself. This is the first step in reconnecting with your greatness. When you refuse to admit your weaknesses, you are also out of touch with your real strengths. Stay with a question throughout a day. Put down your observations in a daily journal. Journaling clarifies your insights. It also allows you to gauge your progress when a similar situation occurs in the future.

Sharing insights with people you trust is a wonderful way to learn about yourself. Partner with one or a group of friends who are willing to take the journey with you. When you share insights with each other, several things happen. By speaking your insights, they become real for you. Other people may also see something about you that you may not have seen and this is a wonderful gift to receive from others. Finally, although the circumstances may be unique to a person who is sharing, the fundamental issues are common among us. So not only do you learn from your own experiences but also from the experiences of others in the group. When you form a sharing group, it is important to create an environment that is safe for people to share. I suggest that you establish the ground rules before you begin, and agree to honor them. There are two ground rules that are essential to creating safety. First, whatever is shared in the group is confidential and does not get out beyond the session. This is a sacred conversation among people who trust each other. Second, when people are sharing, do not judge what they are saying as right or wrong. Allow them to be heard.

Most chapters build upon previous chapters. The best way to get the most out of the book is to go through the chapters in a consecutive manner the first time around. Stay with the questions before moving on to the next chapter. Once you've gone through the book, go back to any chapter that you want to explore further.

This is a journey to the greatness that you are. Enjoy it. Let's get started!

PART I

OUR CIRCUMSTANCES
AND OUR ROLE IN CREATING THEM

The happiness of your life depends upon the quality of your thoughts.

- *Marcus Antonius (A.D. 86-161)*

Chapter 1

What We See
Is What We Have Our Attention On

My student, Larry, and I were in a meeting one day. We were going over the requirements that he needed to fulfill to complete his degree.

He said to me, "What I am most afraid of is this upcoming preliminary exam."

I said, "Don't worry about the prelims. Your professors will ask you things that a student of biology should know. You are ok, you have taken the appropriate courses, you have done well, and you know a lot from the research that you have been working on for the past two years." Seeing that he still looks worried, I said, "Just trust yourself."

He answered, "That's the problem. I don't trust myself."

I sensed that Larry felt stuck. As objective observers, we can see that Larry is the one creating his problem. We can also see that he can change his thought, "I can't trust myself." But Larry cannot see this. To him, his problem was real and he felt there was nothing he can do about it. The thing is - we all do this. We find ourselves stuck in situations and we feel helpless. It may be a demanding boss, a difficult co-worker, a lazy employee, a spouse who does not listen, an irresponsible child. These situations weigh us down. Seeing no other way, we say, "What's the point? Why bother? There is nothing I can do about this." When we see our circumstances as real and fixed, we resign.

In every person and every situation, there are many possibilities. But **we only see what we have our attention on**. In Larry's case, he sees his untrustworthiness. He always looks to others for answers as to the next step to take in his research project. And yet, knowing Larry, I also see another aspect of him that he does not see. He is a straight-A student, a bright young man who is capable of grasping complex concepts.

Here's an exercise to illustrate my point. Look at the figure below.[©] What do you see at first glance?

Do you see the black vase? Is there anything else you see? For most people, the black vase is all there is. We have been conditioned to put our attention on the black print against a white background. Now shift your attention to the white space. What do you see?

The white space has the mirror images of a woman's profile.

[©] The illustration is from Ralph Strauch's *The Reality Illusion*. Pacific Palisades, CA: Somatic Options (1989), reprinted by permission of the publisher.

Until you put your attention on the white space, however, it is as if this image did not exist for you. It is the same with our lives. When we do not see a possibility, it does not mean that it is not there. We are just not seeing it.

What we have our attention on is a function of our thoughts. If you have a thought that your child is irresponsible, you will see the evidence to support that (see diagram below). This evidence will further reinforce the thought until you are convinced there is no other way this child can be. You become conditioned to see his irresponsible behavior and you relate to your child out of this box that you have put him in. In the meantime, you are blind to all the other possibilities of your child. Imagine that there is this large circle that contains all the possibilities for your child, but those possibilities are outside your field of vision. The only things you can see are those that fit in the box called, " Irresponsible child." **The thoughts we have about others and ourselves form the box that we see from**. What we are seeing and experiencing, is but a speck in the realm of all possibilities, most of which we are blind to. In Part II, we will begin opening ourselves up to these other possibilities. Before we can do that, the next step is to begin to be aware of our thoughts and their impact on our lives.

To summarize:

☆ There are many possibilities, but we only see what we have our attention on.

☆ What we have our attention on is determined by our thoughts.

Questions:

1.) In what situations or circumstances do you feel stuck?

2.) For each situation, what are your thoughts about yourself or about the other person(s) involved?

Chapter 2

Our Circumstances are Perfectly Consistent With Our Thoughts

In the previous chapter, we learned that our thoughts determine what we see or perceive. This is the crux of our role in creating our circumstances: **what we think, determines what we experience and what we can create**. How so? Our thoughts shape our behavior and actions, and the consequences of our actions show up in our lives as our circumstances. Let us say, a person has a thought that he is a failure. Although there are things that he does well, he will take them for granted and instead he will focus on things that he does not do well. Someone may complement him for a job well done, and he answers, "oh no, I goofed up in this other thing." He may not accept opportunities that present a risk of failing. Consequently, he may not be taken seriously at work. He may stay in a job where he feels safe and comfortable, although he finds it boring and unsatisfying. Fear of failing in relationships may result in him not having committed relationships. These circumstances reinforce his belief that he is a failure, and the vicious circle goes on as shown in this diagram:

Thoughts ⟶ Behavior and Actions ⟶ Circumstances

Our thoughts are powerful. They form images in our minds and all that we do, are consistent with those images. The Buddha (563-484 B.C.) said:

> All that we are is the result of what we have
> thought. The mind is everything. What we
> think, we become.[3]

Whatever we have in our life is perfectly consistent with our thoughts. This includes our jobs, the quality of our relationships, people we have (or don't have) in our lives, our finances, our self-expression, etc. You are probably wondering, why would a reasonable person have thoughts that do not serve them? Here's why – we are unaware of these thoughts, especially the ones that we have made up as children. Situations happened in our childhood that impacted us, and our thoughts or interpretations about those events formed our fundamental beliefs about ourselves and the world. For example, I grew up in a home with six children, and my father made a modest income. I remember my parents often had fights about money. I made the decision that what I wanted was not that important. Whenever I wanted to have something other children had, I did not ask my parents for it. This thought shaped my actions and interactions with others. I did not ask for

---

[3] Buddha, quoted by Gary W. Fenchuk. *Timeless Wisdom, A Treasury of Universal Truths.* Virginia: Cake Eaters Inc. (2000).

what I wanted. I supported other people well, but I did not ask for support. It also held me back from doing what I really wanted to do. Although I had wanted to write this book for a long time, I couldn't do it until I realized that my thought about it was, "I have nothing important to say." My circumstances were consistent with the thought, "I am not important." I experienced life as a burden. I had too much work to do, trying to do everything by myself. Projects that were important to me were not getting done. Because I did not speak up, I did not get what I want, and I did not feel heard and appreciated.

We have forgotten that we made up these thoughts. What's worse is that although they are in the background shaping our behavior, we are unaware of them. Until we become aware of our thoughts about ourselves, we are at their effect. They run us. What we can create is limited by what fits those images. Have you ever wondered why you keep running into the same problems in life although you are trying hard to fix them? We try hard to fix the circumstances and what we really need to do is to become aware of the source of our actions that produce the results we are getting in life. Becoming aware of these thoughts is the first step to changing any behavior.

There are questions we can ask ourselves to become aware of these thoughts. One question is, what are you afraid people you care about will think of you? Or, what do you try hard to prove about yourself? The opposite of that is what you are avoiding. We will go out of our way to prove that we are not what we are afraid people will think about us. I tried so hard to prove I was important by taking on more work, and accomplishing "important" things. I felt that I had to be doing something all the time. My friend, Joey is a research scientist and supervises students and laboratory technicians. Friendly, easy-going, and soft-spoken, he is well liked by people. In fact, Joey is too nice, all the time, even when his people are not performing their jobs. Instead of telling his employees that their performance is not up to par, he says nothing and tries to make up for their inadequacies by doing their work. When I asked him what he is most afraid people will think about him, he replied that he never wants to be thought of as mean and cruel like his father. Joey cannot allow himself to get angry with people. The images of mean and cruel are in his mind and it is a threat for him to be like those images. His need to be nice all the time affected his effectiveness with people. He couldn't depend on other people and always ended up doing everything himself. He is overworked and not as productive as he can be.

These thoughts or their consequences are not necessarily bad. Some of them may serve us at certain times. For example, it has served Joey to be nice and it has served me to be supportive of other people. What gets us in trouble is that we have no freedom to behave or act in other ways that are inconsistent with our images of ourselves, even when those actions are the most appropriate for the situation. We feel stuck when we act in one, fixed way. Other possibilities are shut out. As a result, our effectiveness in life is severely handicapped. If Joey can allow himself to feel his anger when people are not doing their jobs and express it appropriately, he will be a much more effective supervisor. He may come up with ways of training his employees so that they take responsibility for carrying out their projects. Consequently, they will be trained better, Joey's time will be freed up for other things such as planning for the future of their team, and together they can accomplish greater things. Seeing that the source of my being stuck in writing this book was the thought, "I am not important, and I have nothing important to say," gave me freedom to just write and say whatever I wanted to say, regardless of whether I judged it to be important or not. Whatever we identify ourselves to be is not fixed. It is just a thought.

To summarize:

☆ Our thoughts shape our behavior and actions and the consequences of our actions show up in our lives as our circumstances.

☆ Whatever we have in life is perfectly consistent with our thoughts.

☆ When we are unaware of our thoughts, they run us, and they limit our effectiveness.

☆ Becoming aware of our thoughts gives us freedom to behave differently from the past and opens us up to new possibilities.

Questions:

1.) Use these questions to access thoughts that underlie your behavior and actions:

    a. What are you afraid people will think about you, particularly those you care about (your parents, a partner, boss, children, etc.)?

    b. What do you try hard to prove about yourself?

    c. Think of a specific situation that upset you. It may be recent or it may have happened a long time ago. It may not have been a big upset. It could have been as trivial as your husband asking you to cook while you were reading and it pushed your buttons. What was your thought about the situation or about what the other person said?

2.) In a Table, write down how the thought you came up with shapes your behavior and actions. Write down the consequences of those actions under the column "Life Circumstances and Experiences." The table shows examples for myself and for Joey.

Thought	How it shapes my behavior	Life Circumstances & Experiences
Nora:		
I am not important	I do not ask for what I want. I do not ask for support. I put the needs of others first. I do not speak up. I do not express my gifts.	I do not get what I want. I have too much work to do. My own projects do not get fulfilled. I do not feel heard and appreciated. I feel empty and unfulfilled.

Thought	How it shapes my behavior	Life Circumstances & Experiences
Joey:		
I can't be mean	Always nice. No freedom to be tough. Does not tell his employees what is not working.	He works extra to make up for his employee's deficiencies. Ineffective with people. Low productivity, despite hard work and long hours. No sense of being able to rely on others.
Your name		

3.) Who do you consider yourself to be? In other words, how would you describe yourself? Note that there will be more than one answer to this question. Your answer to the question above forms the predominant thought that underlies most of your behavior. Other thoughts developed from that one. For example, my predominant thought is, "I am not important." In my attempt to prove the opposite of what I am avoiding, I honed in on working all the time and accomplishing. I also consider myself to be my accomplishments. These other thoughts also have their consequences. For me, it is being overworked and not feeling good with slowing down and taking time to play. Write down the behavior and consequences for each of these things that you identify yourself to be.

4.) Do these exercises with a partner. Share your insights. Ask your partner or someone who knows you well how he/she sees or perceives you. What do they see about you? If you ask for feedback, make sure you are willing to hear what is said without taking it personally. Listen to whatever is offered as a gift.

Chapter 3

Are The Pay-Offs Worth It?

The thoughts that you have begun to uncover in Chapter 2 are deeply ingrained in you. They are so deep that you mistake them for your identity. That is why they are hard to see. Becoming aware of these thoughts is like trying to see your face without a mirror. It is impossible! Stepping back as we did in the previous chapter is a way to begin to gain awareness of those thoughts. These deeply ingrained thoughts, which we will refer to from hereon as "habitual thoughts," have resulted in habitual patterns of behavior. The behavior then produced whatever circumstances you have in your life up to this point.

The good news is that awareness of our habitual thoughts is the first step in changing a behavior that no longer serves us. The bad news is that we never get rid of these habitual thoughts. We can, however, learn to shift to empowering thoughts when we have awareness of what is shaping our behavior in the present. It is hard to get rid of these habitual thoughts because no matter how disempowering, they are familiar, comfortable, and they bring us pay-offs. While habitual thoughts and patterns have gotten us this far in life, they also hold us back from realizing new possibilities. When we feel stuck, unable to move forward, we are at the effect of habitual thoughts and patterns. This then is the cost.

In this chapter, we will explore both the pay-offs and costs for keeping a habitual thought. As you read, think of how it relates to you.

Pay-offs

The dictionary defines pay-off as an unconscious or hidden benefit of a negative thought pattern or action. Habitual thoughts and patterns fulfill psychological needs that are part of being human. These needs are:

1.) **To be right or avoid being made wrong.** It is a natural reaction for human beings to want to be right. Just look at your own experience – if someone points out something wrong in you or that you did, don't you become defensive? To be made wrong pushes our buttons. We will do anything to be right. And there are different ways people do this. Blaming others is one. For example, if you are in a messy relationship, it is easier to point a finger at the other person, than to admit your own role in the matter. To admit, "I made a mistake," is like saying, "I am wrong."

Others will sabotage their own success. If a person's habitual thought and identity is "I am a failure," who would be wrong if that person becomes successful? He would be! One way I get to be right is by not asking for what I want. You see, if I ask for what I want and get it, then I would be wrong in my habitual thought that "what I want does not matter."

Some people will go to extremes to prove they are right. Religious fanatics will kill themselves to prove they are right in their beliefs and to make those who do not share their beliefs wrong. Suicide is the ultimate form of the statement "You are wrong!" It is proving someone wrong - it may be parents, a spouse, children, or society.

How are you being right?

2.) To dominate or avoid being dominated. Domination is a way to control others and get what we want. There are different styles of domination, and some are more obvious than others. The book, "Celestine Prophecy" describes these styles.[4] Some people control others by intimidation. Other styles are less subtle. Some people feel sorry for themselves when they don't get what they want, and then make others feel guilty. Making people feel guilty is a great way to control. When your child cries because you didn't buy the toy that he wanted, doesn't that make you feel guilty and want to buy the toy? Still other people dominate by being aloof and mysterious. These are people who go into a corner and withdraw when they are unhappy. Others around them are left wondering what they have done wrong.

What is your style of domination?

---

[4] James Redfield. *The Celestine Prophecy:* An Adventure. New York: Warner Books (1994).

Costs

No matter how great the pay-off seems, there are costs. Huge costs. We trade or give up something to be right or to dominate. The costs show up in four areas of our life:

1.) **Health and well-being.** People will give up their life to be right. There are other, more subtle ways that people sacrifice their well-being. People who are driven to succeed will take on enormous tasks at the expense of their health and well-being. They work constantly, with no down time, or no time to exercise. The costs to health may be in the form of hypertension, heart attacks, being overweight or looking older beyond their years.

When you are out to prove something, you are at the effect of a habitual thought. My friend Roger was out to prove he is "Mr. Wonderful". He was always smiling, pleasant, and upbeat. When asked how he was doing, his answer was an automatic "wonderful!" When I met him, I had no idea of the seriousness of problems that he faced in life. His daughter committed suicide several years before. He was battling kidney cancer when I met him. In the book, "Heal Your Life", Louise Hay showed the relationship between our thoughts and physical illnesses.[5] Hay associated cancer with deep hurt, and longstanding resentment, while kidney problems are associated with disappointment and anger. Upon looking carefully and honestly at his situation, Roger admitted that he had been harboring anger

[5] Louise L. Hay. *You Can Heal Your Life.* California: Hay House Inc. (1987).

and resentment for years at the suicide of his daughter. It was only then that he allowed himself to express the suppressed anger. Although his prognosis was not good, to his doctors' surprise, the cancer went into remission. Today Roger is well and enjoying life to the fullest.

2.) Relationships. People will trade their relationships, particularly with family members, to keep a habitual thought and pattern. A person driven to succeed may spend all his time and energy on work and then come home tired and drained, with no energy left for his children and wife. I used to think (and discovered that most people do too) that relationships with those closest to me do not need time. I assumed that because I lived with my husband, he should know me and I should know him. Relationships, like anything else worth having in life, take time and energy to develop.

People are willing to give up relationships to be right. I read a story about a young man who had a very rich father. On his college graduation day, he expected to get a brand new car as a gift from his father. Instead his father handed him an envelope. Deeply disappointed, he thought, "He does not care about me. He never gives me what I want." At that he left home, and never spoke to his father again. His father tried to reach him. He wrote him letters and sent messengers. The son did not respond. Years later, the father died. The son did not come for the funeral. His life went on, he got married and had children of his own. One day while he was going through his stuff, he found a book with the envelope from his father, inserted in it. When he opened the envelope, do you know what he found? A key to a car that his father bought for his graduation present.

When your relationships are not working, usually you are being right about something. When you take what your partner or parent tells you personally, look at what you are being right about. Notice that when you are in a conversation to prove that the other person is wrong, you get a feeling of "high" from an adrenaline rush. It may feel good for awhile, but is it worth giving up a relationship for?

3.) Self-expression. What are you afraid people will think about you? A thought that says, "I should be something", to prove the opposite of what you're afraid people will think about you robs you of your natural self-expression. You put up a front, an image that you want others to see. The problem is, the longer you keep up that front, you lose a sense of who you are, what you love to do, what gives you enjoyment and brings fulfillment.

For example, out of fear that people will think I am insignificant, I worked hard to appear successful (and important). I accumulated accomplishments. I was rigid, in control of my emotions, and independent. And yet what was natural to me was a soft and gentle way of being. I saw possibilities in human beings and yearned to write a book on this subject for a long time, but it had no place in the image I had to keep up. Pleasure in whatever accomplishments I had was short-lived. Soon I was back to feeling empty and hungry for more. There was no sense of satisfaction or fulfillment.

I am of the opinion that the biggest cost to keeping a habitual thought and pattern is the suppression of our natural self-expression. Our self-expression brings us aliveness. To not express our gifts and our authentic selves, deadens our senses until we do not know anymore what brings us joy. Not knowing who we are and what we care about causes dis-ease within ourselves. We cannot stand to be alone with ourselves. We run away from the loneliness by burying ourselves in busyness, endless activities, alcohol, or hours and hours watching television. People may leave a job, a home, or a marriage that they think is the cause of their unhappiness, only to end up with the same problems with different people. We cannot run away from ourselves.

4.) Finances. Our finances are a direct reflection of the thoughts we have about money and our relationship to it. The story of Robert Kiyosaki's two Dads, in his book "Rich Dad, Poor Dad"[6] is an excellent demonstration that whatever money people have is consistent with their thoughts or conversations about it. Robert's real father, whom he called Poor Dad, was highly educated and a high-ranking official with the public school system. Although his Dad made a good income he acted "poor." When the young Robert wanted to buy something, his father would

---

[6] Robert T. Kiyosaki. *Rich Dad, Poor Dad.* New York: Warner Books (2000).

say "we can't afford that." He always told Robert, "you have to work hard for money." Rich Dad was Robert's best friend's father. He was not highly educated and while he did not make a lot of money in the beginning, he never considered himself as poor. "Poor," he said, is a state of mind, while "broke" is a temporary condition. When his own son, Mike, wanted to buy something, he would say, "how can we afford that?" While the conversation "we can't afford that" shuts down possibilities, "how can we afford that?" opens up possibilities. Rich Dad's conversation about money was that "you make it work for you, you don't work for it". Privy to both Dads' lives and how they unfolded, Robert watched his father struggle with his finances throughout his life, regardless of how much he was making. When he lost his job with the school system he went bankrupt and died a poor man, consistent with his thoughts. Rich Dad, on the other hand, became richer with time, eventually becoming one of the wealthiest men in Hawaii.

What are your thoughts about money? My own conversation was, "there is not enough money." This was a conditioning I grew up with as I watched my parents struggle to stretch my father's monthly income until the next paycheck. My own experience of money has been that there was not enough. Even when I got promoted and received salary increases, still there was not enough money to buy everything that I wanted.

I hear many people say, "If I become a millionaire, my problems will be solved." We have heard of people winning the Lotto and becoming instant millionaires, only to be poor again in a few years. You see - it is never about the amount of money that you have. It is about your own relationship with money. I have a friend who became a millionaire through business, having started with nothing. Though she is now financially well off, she never outgrew her scarcity thinking about money. Since most of her money is in the stock market, she lives in constant fear and anxiety that she will lose all her money if the market crashes.

The western culture has a paradigm that a person's value is measured by the amount of money that he/she makes. In science, a paradigm serves as a model for how things work, and forms a framework for carrying out research. Societies have paradigms too, but we forget that they are simply models and not reality. If we buy into society's paradigms without examining them, they run us. A person with the thought, "I am a failure," will not feel deserving of having a lot of money. He may get a job that will not pay well. Or get into business that never becomes profitable.

The thoughts we made up about ourselves are so powerful that they shaped whatever we have in our lives today. These four areas of costs are interrelated. An impact in one area will typically affect the others. For example, your health and vitality affect your self-expression. Your self-expression affects what you do and how much you make. Your finances impact your relationships. Your relationships impact your well-being. And so on.

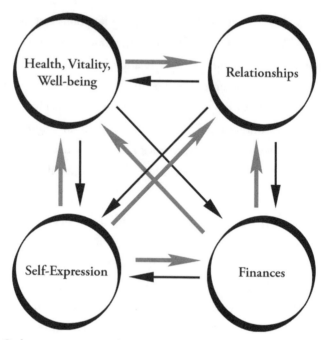

Only you can see what it is costing you to keep a habitual thought or pattern in place. As you answer the questions below, be specific. In relationships, for example, who is the person? What is your experience of the relationship with this person? Get in touch with what the pattern is costing you in real terms. This means to feel it in your heart and body. If you really connect with the costs, you will be in tears grieving for what you are missing out on. This is what it takes to choose to give up the pattern. No matter how difficult it may be to look at the costs, keep in mind that these are consequences of habitual thoughts, which run us. We have a choice with our thoughts, but first, we have to be willing to honestly look at the costs of keeping these habitual patterns in place.

To summarize:

⭐ Habitual thoughts and patterns give us pay-offs. We get to be right and we get to dominate.

⭐ There are also costs for keeping a habitual thought and pattern. The costs are in areas of health and well-being, relationships, self-expression, and finances.

⭐ Habitual thoughts and patterns have taken you this far. They also hold you back from moving forward. If you say you are ready to move on and realize your possibilities, are you willing to give up the pay-offs?

Questions:

1.) Go back to your answers for the questions in Chapter 2. For each pattern of behavior or action, look at the pay-offs. How do these make you right or avoid being made wrong? How does it allow you to dominate or avoid being dominated?

2.) Now look at the costs of your habitual thoughts and patterns. Be specific. Feel the impact that the thought has had in your health and well-being, relationships, finances, and self-expression.

3.) If you do not change, what would your life look like 5 years from now? 10 years from now? 20 years from now?

Expose yourself to your deepest fear. After
that, fear has no power… you are free.

- James Douglas Morrison

Chapter 4

What You Resist, Persists

At this point, you are probably asking, "how do I fix this?" When we find ourselves in a situation that we do not want, our normal reaction is to want to fix it or change it. It may seem to work for awhile but soon the problem is back again. A woman who is fed up with being married to a jerk will divorce her husband and marry a wonderful man. In a few years, it appears that the wonderful man turns out to be another jerk.

There is a law of nature at work here. **What you resist, persists.** The more you resist something, the stronger it becomes. Bodybuilders use resistance to build up muscles. It is the same with creating our circumstances. What we resist has our attention. And what we have our attention on is what we keep getting and creating more of, out of all possibilities. Fixing or changing something is a form of resistance. It is a statement that there is something wrong with it and you do not want it. Anything that you avoid, fight, run away from, or say you are against, are all forms of resistance. Do you notice that fighting war only breeds more wars?

Now, this sounds like a dilemma. We created our experiences by our thoughts and when we try to change that experience that we don't want, we only get more of it.

With the tools we have at this point, we can look at this from a different point of view. Remember, that situation that you don't want is a result of a thought. It is just a thought. Moreover, it is your own creation, your brainchild. Realizing this, you have the power to choose empowering thoughts. But what do you do when you are in the middle of a problem, or an upset?

When things are not going your way, you get into a "bad" mood. It may be one of frustration, desperation, rage, sadness, etc. A mood is always preceded by a thought. When you find yourself in a bad mood, instead of focusing on the mood, stop and ask yourself, "What is my thought about this situation? What is my thought about myself, or the other person?" When you realize that whatever you are going through is the result of a thought, you have a choice about it.

Instead of resisting the thought, practice embracing it. Embrace does not mean to agree with it. Think of it, when you embrace another person, you have an awareness that you are separate from that person. It is the same here, you are simply bringing awareness that the mood you are experiencing came from a thought and that thought is not you. It is separate from you. When you embrace a friend in distress, you are not trying to change that person. You are simply there with your friend, allowing her to feel what she is going through. This is the same with embracing a thought. Just let the thought be there, give it room to be.

When you give something room to be, it disappears. When you tell your small child to stop crying, do you notice that he only cries more? Give him room to cry, and then soon he is playing again.

How do you give room for a thought? First of all, acknowledge that it is there. Do not judge it as good or bad. I have a friend who makes a living by making cold calls on potential customers. Before she picks up the phone she often has the thought that the person on the other line will not want to talk to her and that she is a bother. When she catches herself thinking that, she says, "thank you" to the thought and then she dials the phone number.

When I'm in a meeting and I'm going over in my head how to say what I want to say so I will not look foolish, I speak up and say, "I don't know how to say this and I'm afraid of looking foolish, but I'll say it anyway." By saying this, I've given myself room to speak without the concern for being perfect. Once I put the thought out, it no longer shapes the way I am being as I speak. The things that we don't say, but are in the background, come through loud and clear. Put them out there and they disappear.

I am reminded of a classmate in my college Speech 101 class. The topic she chose to give a speech on was "Fear of public speaking." During her speech, she described what it looks like to be afraid when you're in front of people. She said they include, sweating, fumbling with coins in your pocket, shaky voice. The funny thing was, she was so nervous that she demonstrated all these things she was talking about while she tried to hide her nervousness. Seeing her discomfort, the audience was getting very uncomfortable. Now, if she had an awareness of her thought and said, "As you can see, I am demonstrating all of these for you live today," can you imagine the laughter it would have caused? Every one would have felt at ease, including herself.

To summarize:

⭐ When you want to change, fix, or run away from a situation that you do not want, you will only get more of it. What you resist, persists.

⭐ Realize that a bad mood came from a thought. And the thought is separate from you.

⭐ Embrace the thought. Give it room to be. Acknowledge it or put it out there and it disappears.

Questions:

1.) Think of a specific situation that did not go your way and took you into your typical "bad" mood. How do you describe your mood?

2.) What was your thought about the situation, or yourself, or the other person before you went into your mood?

3.) Relive the situation in your mind. Imagine it happening again. This time, instead of going into your mood, imagine the thought with a body of its own that is separate from you. Embrace it. Acknowledge its presence, without judging it to be good or bad.

4.) The next time you catch yourself thinking the thought that consistently takes you to your mood, experiment with being playful with this thought. You may say, "there you are again."

Or, "thank you, and good-bye." You can also try getting a thing that will symbolize this thought you are avoiding. Put it in your key chain and the next time you catch yourself with this thought, touch this symbol to remind you that it is separate from you.

5.) As you practice catching the thought before you get into an upset, take note of what is opening up for you. When our attention is not on what we are resisting, other possibilities begin to open up for us.

To be blind is bad, but worse it is to have eyes and not see.

- Helen Keller (1880-1968)

Part I

Summary

Life is full of possibilities, but we limit our possibilities by our thoughts. Our thoughts determine what we have our attention on, and that is all that we are capable of seeing. Our thoughts form the box that we live life from and determine what we can create. In Part I, we examined the thoughts that are in the background shaping our behavior and actions, to which we are oblivious. These thoughts become THE truth, leaving us no freedom to be, or act in any other way, that are inconsistent with the images associated with those thoughts. Consequently, we keep getting the same results in life, whether we want them or not. Awareness of these thoughts is the first step in transforming our lives. Rather than resisting the thought, embrace it, give it room to be, and it will let you be. Once you can do this, you now have freedom to choose empowering thoughts that allow you to create new possibilities.

One must have the adventurous daring to accept oneself as a bundle of possibilities and undertake the most interesting game in the world –

making the most of one's best.

- Harry Emerson Fosdick (1878-1969)

PART II

CREATING NEW POSSIBILITIES

First I was dying to finish high school and start college.

And then I was dying to finish college and start working.

And then I was dying to marry and have children.

And then I was dying for my children to grow old enough so I could return to work.

And then I was dying to retire.

And now, I am dying ... and suddenly realize

I forgot to live.

- Author Unknown

Chapter 5

The Principles of Creation

In Part I, we have seen the impact of our thoughts in creating our experiences and whatever we have in life up to this point. If you fast-forward in your imagination to what your future looks like, you can expect that it will be more of the same. You see, the future is not out there somewhere. The future is being created right here as you think and speak.

How do we create a future that is different from our past? A future that is in line with the highest vision of God for us. The book of Genesis lays out for us the fundamental principles of creation. These principles apply to every thing that we manifest in life.

The First Principle Of Creation

Genesis 1 says that in the beginning "the earth was formless and empty...and then God spoke, 'Let there be light' and there was light." (Gen 1:2). Speaking and thinking consist of words. **Every creation begins with a word.** This quote describes the power of words in creation:

> *Words do not label things already there.*
> *Words are like the knife of the carver.*

> *They free the idea from the general form-*
> *lessness of the outside.*
> *As a man speaks, not only is his language*
> *in a state of birth,*
> *But also the very thing about which he is*
> *talking.*

-Edmund Carpenter [7]

Words "free the idea from the general formlessness of the outside." How so? Words clarify for us what we intend to manifest. The words we use call up images in our minds and those images determine what shows up in our world. When you say, "I feel lousy today," you are not merely describing an existing condition, you are also making a declaration of what you will manifest. A declaration is a statement of what is possible. It is invented out of nothing and it becomes a guiding principle. Think of the Declaration of Independence. When the Founding Fathers of the United States of America wrote the Declaration of Independence, it was invented as a possibility for what this country could become. That document became the guiding principle for what this country stood for. It shaped the country into what it is today.

It is the same with our personal declarations – they become the guiding principles for our lives. They shape who we become. When we declare, we are not aware of the impact it has in our lives. Consider the impact of these declarations: "I'm tired," "I'm sick," "I'm overwhelmed," "I have no time," "I have no money," "I can't afford it," "I'm not talented enough," "I'm not good enough,"

---

[7] Edmund Carpenter. *Eskimo Realities.* New York: Holt, Rinehart, and Winston (1973).

"Men can't be trusted," "Teen-agers are difficult." And we're only talking about your life here!

What are your favorite declarations?

The Second Principle Of Creation

All creation takes place in the present moment. Again the book of Genesis sheds light on this. Creation did not take place when God was planning what the world will look like in the future. He was there in the present moment, making the declaration and watching what was happening. We think of creation differently. We set goals and our attention is always to a better future. We say, "Someday when I have money (or when I have time), I will …." You can fill in the blanks. Most of us have one of these declarations.

When our attention is on a better future, we are resisting our present condition. And of course you know what happens. What you resist is what you get more of. And then you wish all the more for a better future. What you get is a vicious circle. And you can't be present to what is going on in life right now.

The saddest thing is that we miss out on what is happening in our lives. We are not here. We are out to lunch most of the time. We live life out of habit, going through the motions while we wait for the future to come. When we live out of habit, we do not think anymore. How many times have you gotten in your car and got to work without awareness of what you were doing? When I was in the gym the other day, a woman was opening up all the lockers in the Women's locker room because she couldn't remember where she put her things just an hour earlier. What passes for thinking is mostly habitual thought. Actually, it is more accurate to say that habitual thoughts have us. They run us. We rarely stop and think anymore if what we are doing is working. Do you ever ask yourself, "Is what I am doing working?"

There is a tale of a young housewife who always cuts the sides of ham before she puts it in the oven to bake. One day, her 5-year old daughter asked her, "Mom, why do you do that?" The woman stopped to think and then said, "You know, Sweetie, that is a good question. Your Grandma always did it this way." The next time the woman saw her mother, she asked, "Mom, why do you cut the ends of the ham before you put it in the oven?" Her mother replied, "I learned that from your grandmother. But come to think of it, I don't know why she did it." So the woman's mother in turn asked her own mother the same question, to which the old woman replied, "I had to. Our ovens were so small then, the ham would not fit." Like the woman in this story, we still do things that we have done even though they no longer work anymore.

Principles Of Creation At Work

Creation is every human being's birthright. We are creating our reality all the time, and for the most part we have done this with no awareness. How do we put the principles of creation to work, to create something that we want?

Creation begins with a declaration. I want to distinguish old, familiar conversations or habitual thoughts from a declaration. The diagram below shows habitual thoughts as the box that we see and experience life from. Habitual thoughts are based on the past.

For example, a decision you made as a child. As such, they come with a package of evidence.

A declaration is shown as a circle, no corners. It is a possibility that you are willing to stand in. What does it mean to "stand" in a possibility? The dictionary defines "stand" as, "to be in a particular condition or state". Also, "to be at a particular point while subject to change or fluctuation." The possibility that you declare determines where you come from in the present moment, regardless of what is happening outside of you. When I declare, "I make a difference", it shapes my behavior here in the present. I may do the same things I have always done, but now my relationship to what I do will be different from before, when I did things out of habit. As such, a declaration does not require evidence. It is not based on the past. It is a statement of what you are being in the present moment. Declarations change the quality of our experience in the present. And consequently, the results that we get will be different.

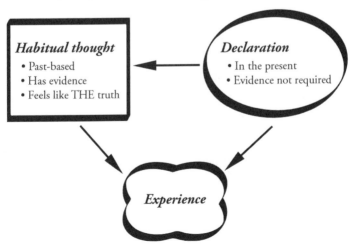

Both habitual thoughts and declarations determine what we have our attention on and what we see, and consequently shape our behavior and our experiences (as shown in the diagram). However, the quality of the experiences will be different. Since a habitual thought comes with evidence, it feels like THE truth. People and situations appear to be fixed and there is nothing we can do about them. A habitual thought leaves us feeling stuck and resigned. We see no other possibility – the habitual thought limits what we are capable of seeing. They act like "filters", eliminating everything that does not fit the thought. A declaration, on the other hand, opens up a new possibility. It allows you to see opportunities you have not noticed before.

The key to making a declaration is that it is generated in the present. This means you are speaking a possibility in the present. Let's experiment with this. We will practice making a declaration in the following format:

"I am a possibility for _____."

Fill in the blank with something that you want to experience in your life right now. Then ask yourself, what does it feel like to be that? What does it look like? For example, if I declare, "I am a possibility for abundance," what that would feel like for me right now is contentment, overflowing with love, support, and resources, feeling secure rather than fearful. By being present to the declaration that I made, I generate the feelings that would come with that condition. Going through my day coming from that state of mind that I generated would create a different experience for me. I may notice things I would not normally notice, like the gorgeous weather, the flowers, and birds singing. I may see the blessing that my job brings to me, it allows me to use my gifts and contribute to others. I begin to notice how people want to support me succeeding in life.

Watch that when you make a declaration, it is not a reaction to something that you do not want. For example, "I do not want to be poor", or "I do not want to fail", are also declarations, although stated in the negative. These negative declarations put your attention on what you do not want. And guess what happens? You get more of it! They also engender fear or whatever mood you get into whenever you are not getting what you want.

Our declarations generate the mood and energy that we come from in the present. This will in turn attract the same energy back to us. When we generate positive energy, we begin attracting those things that we want to create.

I put it in this format (I am a possibility for …) to remind you that it is a possibility. You see, when you create a declaration for a new possibility, it will not feel right. It is unfamiliar and has no evidence. It feels made up. And so what! Habitual thoughts and conversations were once made up. But because these thoughts have filtered what we were able to see in the past, we bought into these thoughts and took them to be the truth.

A word of caution. A declaration today can be a habitual thought tomorrow (notice the arrow from declaration to habitual thought in the diagram). When it becomes a memory, you begin looking for evidence. When you first fall in love with a person, you experience wonderful feel-good sensations like excitement and a pounding heart, in his/her presence. When those feelings go away with time, then you begin to question whether you really love that person. When you declare, "I love you," you are not looking for evidence. Your declaration shapes how you see and interact with the person. Your attention turns to those qualities that you appreciate and love about him/her.

When a declaration turns to a habitual thought, it becomes THE truth. As you look for evidence and see the opposite of what you declared, you become disempowered. My friend Jay declared, "I am abundant", and in the beginning felt good about it. Over time, as he continued saying this, he began looking for evidence. For example, he looked for the same experiences when he first made the declaration. He also began looking for proof that he is getting more money. As he saw the gap between what he had hoped would happen and the present circumstances, he became disheartened and began to think, "Who am I kidding? This is not working. "

Remember this: **declarations do not require evidence.** Evidence is in the past. The impact of a declaration is in the present moment. Your power lives in the present moment. As you think and speak in the present, you are creating your future. To change the results you're getting in life, the present is all you have to work with. Be present to your thoughts and conversations. Awareness of a habitual thought will remove its hold on you. When you catch yourself in a disempowering habitual thought, you have a choice to shift to a declaration that empowers you in the present.

To Summarize:

☆ The future is being created as we think and speak in the present moment.

☆ Creating a new future begins with a word (or string of words), a declaration.

☆ Creation takes place in the present.

☆ A declaration is not based on evidence. It is a statement of a possibility that you are willing to stand in, in the present.

☆ Declarations shape what we see and experience, and who we become.

Questions:

1.) Pay attention to your thoughts and conversations today. What kinds of declarations do you make?

2.) Create a declaration for something that you want to experience in your life, using the format "I am a possibility for …" Focus on the uplifting feelings that becoming your declaration engenders.

3.) Be present to your declaration as you go through your day. Take notice of the following:

a. How is this changing the way you are being, that is, how

you speak, act, and respond to people and situations?

b. How are other people responding to you?

c. What is showing up for you?

d. How is this different from what you've gotten before?

4.) Be aware when a declaration turns to THE truth, and when you have thoughts that say, "Who am I kidding?" Or, "I'm only fooling myself." Or, "This is not working." Without resisting these thoughts, acknowledge they are there. All that is happening is that you are looking for evidence (which is in the past). Practice bringing yourself back to the present moment and connect with your declaration. Shifting to an empowering thought will not be easy in the beginning, but do not get discouraged. Being able to take notice when you are having disempowering thoughts (and they are not your reality) is what being in the present looks like. Acknowledge yourself whenever you catch yourself having a disempowering thought.

Chapter 6

To Be Cause In The Matter

One of the most powerful declarations we can stand in is this: **I am cause in the matter.** This is saying, "I created this situation, and if it is not working, I have the power to create something else."

For most of us, this is not the way we think of our circumstances. Generally, we act as if we are at the effect of other people or circumstances. We are like billiard balls innocently sitting in our places on the table, and then the cue ball comes along, and in the pocket we go. This prevalent way of thinking has made us a culture of blamers. When something happens to us, we look to see who we can blame. We've heard all kinds of stories in the media. A man who buys coffee from a big burger chain store scalds himself and sues the company. Celebrities write books exposing their abusive parents and providing explanations for their present behavior. Lawyers use an abusive childhood to defend criminal activities of their clients.

When you declare that you are cause in the matter, you are owning your responsibility for your thoughts, actions, and choices. Instead of looking out there, you look at your role. This does not mean to put blame on yourself. The word "responsibility" is usually associated with blame and burden. For example, when your boss says, "Who's responsible for this," what is your first thought? Most likely it is something like this: "Uh-oh, something's wrong." Something is wrong and someone is to blame for it. Naturally, if this is what responsibility means, we don't want it. This is not what I mean by responsibility in this context.

Owning responsibility in what you have created is a gift that you give to yourself. Just imagine the power you give yourself when you say, "Yes, I can see how I created that and seeing this, I can create something else." When you own the responsibility, you are no longer at the effect of other people and circumstances. You are in charge of what you create in your world. Instead of being at the effect of the cue ball, you are the cue ball!

This is not to say that things that are beyond our control do not happen in the world. They do. Accidents, death, violent crimes, and catastrophes happen. And even in these situations, we can choose to take the point of view that we are responsible for how we respond. Powerful people use the difficult times to move themselves to doing things they have never done before. Candy Lightner, a woman whose daughter was killed by a repeat drunk driver, started the movement called "Mothers Against Drunk Drivers" (MADD)[8] in 1980. Her aim was to save other children from death or injury resulting from drunk driving. Today, there are 600 chapters in the U.S. and they have been influential in the passing of many laws pertaining to drunk driving.

Even in situations that seem so big and beyond us, like world hunger, we can choose to take responsibility. When we blame poli-

---

[8] http://www.madd.av.org/

ticians and greed for world hunger, it does not change anything, and we feel disempowered. But if we took the point of view that we are responsible, we can start looking at our own habits of consumption, and how much we waste. Perhaps we will begin to explore ways to save on food expenses and send money to those in need.

What does it look like when you take responsibility for making your life work? When there is an undesirable situation that keeps recurring in your life, ask yourself, "Who am I being that this keeps showing up?" Years ago, a neighbor told me that she has been hit eight times by reckless drivers within the last three years. She said, "Everywhere I go, whether here in New York or in other places, I come across reckless drivers. This last time, it happened while I was visiting my niece in a small town in Colorado." She couldn't see that the people and places had changed, and she was the common denominator. Now if she was willing to look at her role in these accidents, she might have realized that she had not been paying attention to the traffic light, or maybe she had problems with her vision, or whatever it might have been that she could have done something about. It seems obvious to us that the first place to look would be with her. And yet, in our own recurring problems, we could not see or refuse to see our role in them. We blame others, and then we get to be right. This is a huge pay-off, and some people would choose this over having power to be the cause and creator of what they have in life. When we are blaming, there is something that we are not taking responsibility for.

To summarize:

⭐ The declaration, "I am cause in the matter," is to take responsibility for your thoughts, actions, and choices. This takes you from feeling like a victim to being the creator of your experience.

⭐ When you are blaming, there is something that you are not taking responsibility for.

Questions:

1.) Think of a problem that keeps recurring in your life. Ask yourself, "Who am I being that this keeps showing up?" For example, if you keep getting into an argument with your teen-age daughter, what are your thoughts about her? How does your thought shape your behavior (who you are being)?

2.) Standing in the declaration that you are cause in the matter, ask yourself, "Do I want this result?" If you honestly do not want it anymore, what result do you want?

3.) What can you think and do differently in the present that is in line with the result that you want?

Chapter 7

Responsibility For Making
Our Relationships Work

D o you ever notice that many of the challenges you deal with involve relationships with other people? It may be relationships with those closest to you, your partner, children, parents, or people with whom you do business.

A powerful declaration to stand in when it comes to relationships is this: **I am 100% responsible for making the relationship work**. Yes, you heard it right – 100%, not 50%. This means that you are putting 0% responsibility on the other person. Now, this does not mean letting other people step on you, or not having expectations in your relationships. What this means is that you are giving yourself the power to make this relationship work instead of having the outcome of a relationship depend on what the other person does.

I know – it does not make sense. There are sayings such as, "it takes two to tango," and "it is a two-way street," that tell us each person in a relationship should be responsible. This is a valid point of view. The question is, does it work?

The following story illustrates what taking 100% responsibility for making a relationship work looks like:

Diana was cleaning the house. She had guests coming that night. There were piles and clutter strewn around the house. She got to the long table in the formal dining room, which is rarely used for its intended purpose, and saw piles of papers left by Brooke, her 16-year old daughter. She sighed, angrily picked up the papers, and moved them to the bottom shelf in the living room where she dumped all the things she had collected so far.

Brooke came home after school and saw the empty dining table. A frown formed on her face and as she dropped her backpack on the floor, she asked Diana, "Now what did you do with my stuff?!" Diana felt the muscles in her neck tighten. She replied, "I put them on the bottom shelf in the living room, just as you had them piled here." Brooke was crying, as she said, "You always mess up my stuff!"

By now, Diana was ready to lash back. She wanted to say, "You ungrateful kid! You never appreciate anything that I do!" Before the words came out, she stopped. In the last few months, she and her daughter have argued over different things. It seems they can no longer carry on a conversation without ending up fighting and both feeling bitter and resentful. At that moment, she asked herself, "What am I doing that Brooke is responding to me this way?"

Diana spoke softly, "Brooke, you are right. I did mess with your things by moving them. I thought it would be ok as long as I kept them in the same order that you had them. Tell me, what is it that so upsets you? What did I do that did not work for you?"

In between sobs, Brooke said, "You knew I would be here before the guests arrived. Why didn't you wait for me?" And then she added, "Mom, I feel that you do not trust me. You think I am irresponsible and I cannot pick up after myself."

Diana was not able to speak. It was true, she has thought of

Brooke as an irresponsible teenager. In fact, just a few hours ago, she picked up Brooke's papers to prove once again how irresponsible her daughter is. She realized that all the arguments they had in the past involved this issue. Diana said, "I hear what you're saying. I have behaved in the past as though you are irresponsible. I am sorry. And that is not you. You are a responsible and dependable person. From now on, I will interact with you that way." Brooke put her arms around Diana, and said, "Oh Mom. Thank you. Yes, you can depend on me." They held each other for a long time.

Diana took responsibility for the outcome of this situation, an outcome that is in line with having a loving relationship with her daughter. She did the following:

1.) Diana put the problem on her side. It could have been easy to point a finger at her daughter and say, "if these papers are so important to you, then why don't you put them in a place where no one will touch them." Instead, she puts the responsibility on her side and asks Brooke, "What did I do that did not work for you?" To put the problem on our side in the midst of a conflict takes heroic effort. This is difficult, and it is not an automatic reaction. It is a choice that we make in the moment when we give higher priority to making a relationship work than to be right.

2.) Diana made it safe for Brooke to open up when she said, "You are right." This is not about giving in. Diana was willing to see that Brooke's point of view was valid and by saying she is right, she created a safe space for Brooke to open up. Remember, the human tendency is to prove we are right or avoid being wrong. Since Diana took care of Brooke's safety, she was able to speak openly.

3.) Diana listened. Can you imagine how hard it is to take feedback about ourselves that is not working for the other person, without taking it personally? It takes courage to sit and listen without defending and justifying ourselves. But it is worth it. When another person gives you honest feedback, what they are giving is a gift. Most people are not willing to give honest feedback unless they care about you and the relationship. No matter what the style of the person is, whether they're angry or nice about it, you can listen for the gift that is being given.

4.) Diana accepted her responsibility in how she has thought of her daughter. More importantly, she made a new declaration, "You are a dependable person." The labels or declarations we have for people create the space that they can show up in. Although each person has many possibilities, what you have your attention on is all that you will see in them. As you see them this way, that is what gets reinforced.

We do not need to fix others. We only need to look within and see how we are holding (or seeing) people in our lives. Hold your children as trustworthy and that is what they will be. Hold your employees and co-workers as competent and dependable and that is what they will be. This is one of the most important lessons I learned in working with people. For a long time, I complained about being overwhelmed at work. The more people I hired, the more I had to do. My employees came to me for decisions on what to do with their projects. Things did not move unless I pushed them. And then one day it hit me. The way I have thought of my staff is that no one can possibly know more than I do, and that is exactly what I got. When I realized this, I talked to each one of them. I said, "I just realized that I have been interacting with you as though you cannot know more than I do. I am no longer willing to interact with you that way. To continue interacting with you that way does not serve you, or me. You are an excellent scientist, and that is why I hired you. From now on, I will work with you as a partner in this project. I will depend on your knowledge and skills while I support you by providing the resources to move your project." Each one of them left my office standing taller and looking more confident than when they came in. That conversation changed them. They began to own their projects and lead, rather than follow. We train people how to interact with us. In this conversation with my employees, I took responsibility for my role in how I trained them to interact with me. Moreover, I took responsibility for retraining them in how to interact with me. Be aware that when we start doing things differently without telling others what we are up to, people become suspicious. By sharing my insights about the impact of my actions on their performance, and by telling them how I wanted to change, I included them in the conversation, and they were not left guessing what I was up to.

What if you hold a person as trustworthy (or responsible, competent, etc.) and they do something that is opposite to that? What do you do? Let us say, you hold your children as trustworthy and then your daughter is caught shoplifting. Do you blow up and condemn her? Or do you keep quiet and tolerate? Neither action will result in your daughter becoming a truly trustworthy person. Continue holding her as trustworthy when you tell her that such a behavior is not acceptable. Remind her who you see her to be – someone trustworthy. Hold her in that space as you allow her to tell you what led to this behavior. Remember, whatever people do, comes from thoughts they have about themselves and others. When you put your attention on their possibilities, then they will begin to step into that. Holding a person as already transformed is different from tolerating his/her behavior. Remember that our responsibility is to make the relationship work for the other person and for us.

To summarize:

☆ In order to take responsibility for a relationship working, put 100% responsibility on your side for the outcome of a relationship.

☆ The way we hold people determines how they show up for us. Take responsibility for the thoughts you have about others. Your thoughts will determine how they show up for you.

Questions:

1.) Think of a person, a group, or organization that you are blaming for something that is not working for you. Ask yourself what it is you may not be taking responsibility for in your relationship with this person or group.

2.) Think of a specific situation that resulted in an upset with another person. You can use a situation that you have used in previous chapters, or you can use another situation, as long as you are still in an upset over that situation. Divide the page into two columns. On the left-hand column, write down what happened as objectively as you can. That is, write down the facts – when, where, who are the people, what was said, ("he said," and then "I said…" and so on.), etc. On the right-hand column, write down your thoughts or interpretations about yourself, the other person, or what he/she did to you. Compare the facts (that is, what happened, what was said, etc.) with your thoughts and interpretations. Notice that it is your thoughts and interpretations that caused you to be upset, not what actually happened. For example, I sent an e-mail message to a colleague requesting a meeting with him. I wanted to ask for his assistance in my research project. I checked my e-mails and there was no response from him. I went to his office and when I saw him, I said, "Hi Dan." He looked at me and said, "I saw your e-mail and I am busy right now. There is something I need to finish." I immediately went to my mood, which is frustration. My thought was, "I am not important to him." It was my interpretation of what he said that upset me. He never said, "You are not important to me." He was simply busy and needed to finish something, just as he said.

3.) See the situation from the point of view of the other person.

Imagine what it felt like to be in his/her shoes given what was going on in his/her life at that time. In the example above, I began to imagine what must be going on in Dan's life given what I knew about him. He is a scientist whose salary is paid from grant money, and so he has to write grants all the time. I imagined he must have been writing a grant with an upcoming deadline. If I were in his shoes, I would have done the same thing. I began to have compassion for what he must be going through. And I realized it was not about me. He simply needed to take care of things that were more important to him.

4.) What new thoughts or interpretations can you come up with that would empower you in your relationship with this person? I chose to come from the interpretation that Dan simply needed to take care of things important to him, and that he also wanted to support me. I gave him room to be, and stopped bugging him. When I met him in the hallway, I said "hi", and asked how he was doing. I realized that I have not talked to him for more than six months. I didn't know what was going on in his life. We reconnected at that moment. The next day, he came to my office and asked how he could support me. When I chose to not take personally what Dan said, my energy and attitude toward him changed. Instead of focusing on what I was not getting, I chose to connect with him first. And he became more open to supporting me when he felt that I was concerned about him.

Chapter 8

The Truth Will Set You Free

The story of Diana and Brooke in the previous chapter brings up an important principle in transforming any relationship. When Brooke said to her mother, "I feel you do not trust me, and think I am irresponsible," and when Diana said, "I have interacted with you as though you are irresponsible," they were being honest with each other. It could have been easy for Diana to say, "No, I did not say anything like that." At that moment they were both willing to speak what was true for them.

To tell the truth is to be willing to say, **"this is what is so for me."** In other words, it is saying, "This is how I feel about what you did," or, "This is my thought about what you did." It is not about right or wrong. It is about being open and honest. It takes guts to tell the truth. This is what it took for you to answer the questions with honesty in the previous chapters.

Telling the truth is a critical step in freeing ourselves from the bondage of habitual thoughts that keep us disempowered and stuck. Before we can create new possibilities, we must be willing to first face the current status of our lives, and embrace it (Chapter 4). From this place of acceptance, we can go for that which we want to create anew.

To tell the truth is more than the act of speaking. When we

declare the possibility of telling the truth, it becomes a way of being. You see, we do not give much thought to lying. In fact, we say things like, "What the other person doesn't know won't hurt him." So we hide or omit things to protect ourselves or the other person. We even have a name for this kind of lie – 'white lie', to distinguish it from 'real lies'. There are no degrees of lying. It is just telling the truth or not.

Lying has enormous consequences. When we omit or withhold something from another person, whatever we are not saying shapes the way we interact with him/her. Have you been in a relationship where you feel there is something the other person is not saying? Whatever is not being said is what's occupying the space between you, so that a connected, intimate and authentic relationship is impossible.

Jennie and Jeff have been married for only two years when something happened that started to drift them apart. In the middle of one night, shortly after midnight, the phone rang. Jeff quickly picked it up so that Jennie would not be awakened. Whispering, he said, "Hello." A few minutes later, he said to the person at the other end of the line, "Ok, I'll meet you outside in a few minutes." He got up, put on a sweatshirt and went out. It turned out that Jennie was awake and was listening to the phone conversation. Her heart was pounding as she began to have thoughts in her mind of who it could be. She decided to pretend to be asleep and see who showed up.

When Jeff left the bedroom, rain began to pour. A few minutes later, someone came. Jeff and the other person got in the back seat of the car, which was parked right in front of their bedroom. Jennie's heart sank. Jeff was with another woman. Although Jennie could hardly make out what she looked like, she could see that the woman had hair that came down to her shoulders. Jennie cried in bed. When Jeff came back, she still pretended to be asleep. She did not say anything the next day, or the day after, or the week or months after. In fact, she pretended that she didn't know. But their relationship changed from that day. They stopped making love. Jennie started gaining weight. In two years, she gained 35 pounds. She stopped taking care of herself and the home, and became very critical of everything that Jeff did. One day, coming home from work and finding Jennie once more in a bad mood, Jeff had had it. He said to Jennie, "Ok. What is going on?"

At first, Jennie said nothing. And Jeff continued, "I don't know what happened. We used to be best friends and now I cannot even talk to you anymore. I cannot go on like this." Jennie burst into tears, as she said, "How dare you! You are cheating on me and pretend like you are so innocent!" "What do you mean?" Jeff was perplexed. Jennie yelled, "Don't deny it! I saw it with my own eyes. You even allowed her to come to our house. You were sitting in the back seat of the car that one night it was pouring. Who is it?", she demanded.

Jeff sighed, "Oh Jennie, that was Frank." Frank was a close friend of Jeff's who sported long hair. That night, Frank found out that his wife was cheating on him and needed to talk to a friend. "He came to talk about his relationship with Lisa. That was a month before they got divorced." And then he said, "Why didn't you tell me all this time? I thought I had lost you forever."

We carry around so many thoughts and interpretations about the people closest to us. We hold back (or withhold) words or thoughts that we think will hurt or destroy them. Guess what, we hurt them more by not saying what is in our heart. We lose precious time and opportunity to connect with them because of a thought that is never said. Choose to tell them the truth out of your love for them, and they will be honored. What is it that you are withholding from someone you love?

Withholding takes away our aliveness. We stuff down resentment and hurt feelings and these physically show up in our bodies as tiredness and heaviness. Physical exhaustion is different from heaviness that is in our chest. When I feel tired and numb (not feeling anything emotionally), this is a sign that I am withholding something, and I ask myself, "What is that I am not saying?" By asking this question, what I typically realize is that something happened that got me upset, but I denied my hurt feelings. This does not mean that you have the right to dump on other people without notice. Remember, when you are 100% responsible for making a relationship work, where you look is within you, not with them. If a thought you have is causing damage to a relationship, a truthful conversation is about owning your responsibility for your thoughts and actions. For example, if your 30-year old daughter keeps coming to you for help with paying her apartment rent, and you are feeling resentful and taken advantage of, look at your thought and behavior that have encouraged her to keep doing this. Out of your commitment to her, you might say something like this, "There is nothing that I want more than to see your life working and to see you happy. And I thought that if I help out with your rent, you will be happy. But then I realized that what I am doing is not serving you or me. I see that my behavior encourages you to rely on someone outside yourself to make your life work. And I, in turn, am feeling taken advantage of. I do not want this anymore to get in the way of our relationship." And then you might see how else you can support her to learn to manage her finances.

Lying also takes you away from the present. When you habitually say, "I'm fine", when someone asks how you're doing regardless of how you are feeling, you are disconnected from the present. Does this mean that we divulge everything about our lives to anyone we meet on the street who asks us how we are doing? No. If you do this, people will think you are crazy and they will avoid you. Taking a stand to tell the truth is to have freedom to be open and honest with people close to us and allow them to see who we are. When you say "yes" to an invitation when you really mean "no", you are left thinking of what to say next to get out of it. When you lie to someone to protect yourself or to look good, you have to remember what you said the next time you see that person. When you say something that you think the other person wants to hear instead of what you really mean, you are left thinking, "was that the right thing to say?"

The rewards of telling the truth are enormous. They include the possibility of a deep and authentic connection with another person, aliveness, and being present in the moment. In other words, you are a whole and complete being moment to moment.

Awakeness

Awakeness is a matter of willingness to be whole,

To be in the present and nowhere else,

A willingness to tell the truth in each moment,

Tell the truth, not like a moral thing,

Tell the truth like it is for you in the present moment.

Then you are free,

There's nothing to remember,

There's nothing to analyze,

"Did I say it right?" Or "Did I say the right thing?"

Having said what is so for you in the present moment,

You are free to move on to the next moment,

A whole, complete, integrated human being,

Living moment-to-moment.

\- Nora Lapitan

To Summarize:

⭐ Telling the truth is the first step in transforming any relationship.

⭐ Telling the truth is a powerful declaration to stand in, in the present moment. It is a way of being.

⭐ What you are omitting or withholding from another person occupies the space between you, making a deep and authentic relationship impossible.

⭐ The rewards of telling the truth include the possibilities for a deep, authentic relationship with another person, aliveness, and being present.

Questions:

1.) Pay attention to your speaking. Catch yourself when you say something to be nice or social.

2.) The next time you catch yourself saying something that you don't mean, practice speaking what you really mean. Let us say, you bumped into a friend and he casually mentions that he has a party that night and asks if you would come, and you said "I'll try", knowing that you have no intention of coming. You may say something like this, "You know what, I take back what I said that I'll try to come to your party. It really will not work for me, I have other plans..."

3.) What are you withholding from people that you love? Usually what we are withholding from those we love are our own judgments and interpretations of their behavior or actions. How are these thoughts and judgments keeping you from having a deep and authentic relationship with them? Are you willing to speak this to him/her? This conversation may not be easy and it may feel very risky. But when you take responsibility for your own thoughts and judgments instead of putting blame on the other person, the reward is a new level of intimacy that has not been possible before.

4.) When you feel tired and heavy, think of a recent situation that resulted in an upset. What did you not say that you are still carrying around?

Part II

Summary

Once we become aware of our thoughts and give them room to be, we can shift to empowering thoughts as we learned in Part II. Our future is being created as we think and speak in the present moment. Creation takes place in the present moment. We can create a future that is different from the past through declarations. A declaration is a stand we take or a place to come from, to empower us in the present moment. A powerful stand to take is "I am cause in the matter." It is saying, "I am the creator of this thought, this action, and this circumstance." We can take this stand in all areas of our lives. In relationships, to take this stand is to say we are 100% responsible for making them work. Telling the truth is another powerful stand that is required in transforming our lives. It is giving ourselves permission to speak what is so for us and to be open and honest in our communication. Telling the truth gives us aliveness in the present and makes it possible to have deep and authentic relationships with ourselves and with others. By being true to ourselves, we begin to know our greatness.

Freedom is the total absence of concern
about yourself…

And the best way to quit being concerned
about yourself

is to be concerned about others.

-Florinda Donner

PART III

LIVING FOR A HIGHER PURPOSE

What we have done for ourselves dies with us.

What we have done for others remains.

We make a living by what we get.

But we make a life by what we give.

- Sir Winston Churchill (1874-1965)

Prologue to Part III

Greatness is every human being's birthright. "Greatness? Me?", you ask. Yes you! Most of us think that greatness belongs to the chosen few who are born with it. Read the following quotation slowly. Let it sink in.

> *Our deepest fear is not that we are inadequate. Our deepest fear is that we are powerful beyond measure. It is our light, not our darkness, that most frightens us. We ask ourselves "Who am I to be brilliant, or just talented, fabulous?" Actually, who are you not to be?*
>
> *You are a child of God. Your playing small doesn't serve the world. There's nothing enlightened about shrinking so that other people won't feel insecure around you. We are all meant to shine as children do. We were born to make manifest the glory of God that is within us. It's not just in some of us, it's in everyone. And as we let our own light shine, we unconsciously give other people permission to do the same. As we are liberated from our own fear, our presence automatically liberates others.*
>
> -Marianne Williamson[9]

---

[9] Marianne Williamson. *A Return to Love*. New York: Harper Collins (1992).

We have been given gifts and insights to share with the world. But unless we are willing to accept (or own) our gifts, they are not real. As we have seen over and over, a possibility does not exist for any of us unless we put our attention on it. There is never a shortage of talents in anyone. It is just an unwillingness to own them. I think the reason we adore people like stars and great athletes is not so much because of their talents but their courage to own their talents and expose themselves to the world. They represent great possibilities that belong to each and every one of us.

The next chapters present pathways for connecting with our gifts and manifesting them in the world. These are not formulas. Nor are these consecutive steps to follow. These are possibilities for us to explore.

Chapter 9

Living For A Purpose
Bigger Than Yourself

When you own your responsibility for choosing thoughts that empower you, you are on your way to creating a life that works for you. However, you will find sooner or later that it is not enough that your own life is working. If this is all that your life is about, pretty soon you will be in the rut once again, going through the motions, feeling that same empty hollow feeling inside.

My intention is to share with you what has worked for me in transforming my life to one that is meaningful and fulfilling. The lessons came from my own experiences as well as from studying the lives of men and women that I consider great. They include people like Martin Luther King Jr, Gandhi, and Mother Theresa.

It begins by inventing a purpose for your life that is beyond your concerns for making a living, paying the bills, and looking good (which includes everything that you want others to think about you). What do I mean by inventing a purpose bigger than yourself? First of all, I do not mean that you quit your job, relocate, or leave your spouse. You can do exactly the same things you are doing now. It is your relationship with these things that will change when you invent a purpose. Creating your purpose gives you an overarching picture of what matters most to you.

It may not be easy for some to define what matters most. Especially when life has become a mere existence, going through the grind day to day. Waking up, going to work, coming home, watching television and going to bed, without awareness of experiencing any of these things. Whether we like it or not, all of us are being used by a purpose. Most people are used by the purpose of surviving, that is, making it through a day, a month, etc. The possibility is to live for a reason beyond our own survival. This is a choice that belongs to each and every one of us.

> *The most basic choice we have in life is whether to expand or contract, whether to bring our creative and expressive energies out into the world in positive or negative ways. No matter what our circumstances, we have the power to choose our directions.*
>
> *In each of us are heroes, speak to them and they will come forth.*
>
> *We have to live and we have to die; the rest we make up.*
>
> - Author Unknown

How do we speak to the hero in us? The last line clues us in – we make it up. We invent a purpose that is beyond making a living and existing day to day. Although a purpose is invented, it is not arbitrary. A purpose reflects what is important to us, what we care most about.

Give yourself a few moments to write down answers to these questions. Write as fast as you can without thinking.

- What do you love?

- What is important to you? What do you care about?

- What do you enjoy the most in the things that you do in a day?

Here are some of my own answers. I love my kids and my family. I love to laugh. I love to watch people giving their heart to what they do, like artists who do what they do with passion. Developing my talents and making a difference are important to me. What I enjoy the most in my job is supporting people with whom I work to develop their gifts, and be the best that they can be. A common theme I saw in answering these questions is my love for bringing out possibilities in people. The purpose I invented for my life is to empower people to access their greatness and express it in the world. I am still doing the same things that I did before I invented this purpose. I am still teaching and doing research at the university. I am still with my husband and kids. What has changed is how I do these things. My purpose guides me in how I relate with my children, husband, students, colleagues, and others on a daily basis. I see people around me as powerful and talented human beings, everyone a work of art in progress. My classes and my research projects have become powerful instruments for me to bring out the best in people. My purpose has guided me in choosing activities in which I invest my time. I no longer have problems saying no to requests that are not in line with my purpose. By inventing a purpose, the quality of my daily existence has changed. Martin Luther King Jr. said "Until you have a cause to die for, you do not know how to live."

Connecting with that which we love is what brings out the hero in us. All of us have fears. That is part of being human. We are afraid of making a mistake, being rejected or looking foolish. A hero is someone who, inspite of the fears, goes on to do what he/she loves. Allow yourself to love what you love, whether it is being in nature, being with children or the elderly, whatever it is that you have a heart for. My friend Bob has a heart for teenagers and young adults. He works as a counselor with the university, helping high school and college kids who are dealing with personal problems. He does what he does with love, not because this is his job. The kids come to his house and have a personal relationship with him. He has impacted so many of these kids' lives and he is one of the most contented people I know.

Over time, your purpose statement may change. Do not worry about it being perfect. It will evolve and become more refined, as you become clearer how you want to make a difference. When you declare that you make a difference, whatever you are doing can become an instrument of service for your fellow human beings. Mahatma Gandhi (1869-1948) said, "the best way to find yourself is to lose yourself in the service of others. "

To summarize:

⭐ We all live for a purpose whether we like it or not. Most of us are used by the purpose of surviving.

⭐ A possibility is to live for a purpose beyond our own survival.

⭐ A purpose is an overarching statement of what matters most to you.

⭐ When you choose to make a difference, whatever you do can become an instrument of service for your fellow human beings.

Questions:

1.) Take time to answer the following questions presented earlier in this chapter:

    a. What do you love?

    b. What is important to you?

    c. What do you enjoy the most in the things that you do in a day?

2.) How do you want to make a difference? Create a purpose statement that encompasses what matters to you and how you want to make a difference. For example, Helen's answers to the questions in no.1 and no. 2 were as follows: a. She loves to sing and play her music for people; she loves challenging sports such as kayaking. b. Family, friends, and people are important to her. c. As a research technician, she loves to support people in their projects. She is a good listener and she loves to support her friends in times of difficulties and challenge. She wants to make a difference by empowering and supporting people. People and relationships are important to Helen. She loves challenges, such as performing music, and challenging sports such as kayaking. The purpose statement that she invented for herself is to empower and support people to take on challenges that are important to them.

3.) Write down your purpose statement and put it places where you will see it many times during the day. Examples are your desk, on your refrigerator door, Palm Pilot, or on your computer screen.

4.) Memorize your purpose statement. Say it and feel it before you take on any task during the day. When faced with a decision, consult it to see if it is in alignment with your purpose.

5.) Write down in your journal how your life purpose is impacting the things you do and experience during the day. Writing it down or sharing it with a friend will make it more real for you.

Chapter 10

Our Dreams Lead Us to Our Greatness

Another way to connect with what we love is by getting in touch with our dreams. What do you dream of accomplishing? Is it to write a song, or sing, or paint, or write poetry or a book? Is it to create a family, or raise your kids to be confident and loving people? Is it to create a beautiful garden in your backyard? Or study languages, travel to other countries? Is it to serve in missions in other parts of the world? No matter how big or small your dream, it is important.

Deepak Chopra said that no matter how trivial our dreams may seem to be, they lead us to God.[10] For me, the presence of "God" within us is seen in the fullest expression of our gifts. Our dreams lead us to our own greatness. As I look at my own history I realize that who I am today has been shaped by the dreams I had. The accomplishment of each one led to the next. In my early '20s in the Philippines, I dreamed of coming to the United States to study for a Master's degree. It led to the next dream, to get a doctorate in Genetics. After that I dreamed of establishing a research program in plant genetics to contribute to the improvement of our food

[10] Deepak Chopra. *The Seven Spiritual Laws of Success: A Practical Guide to the Fulfillment of Your Dreams.* California: New World Library (1994).

crops. As part of creating this research program I soon found myself supervising and leading people, something I have never done before nor have I been trained to do. Yet, I had an interest in understanding what motivates people. I challenged myself to learn how to listen to people's commitments in life and how to support them in achieving their goals. This research led me to the dream of writing a book that would empower people. If I had ignored any of those dreams, my life would have taken a different direction. I don't know what that would have been, but I would not be where and what I am today.

It is easy to set aside a dream and say someday I will work on it, when I am financially independent, or when I retire, or when the kids are grown up, or when I learn to do something. Whatever is your reason for waiting, it will be too late by then. You know why? Your dreams are an expression of what you love and of your deepest commitments in life. When you disconnect from what you love, then you begin to languish and die slowly. Opportunities may present themselves, but if you are simply going through the motions, what are the chances that you'll see them?

The greatest reward you can expect for honoring your dreams is not the accomplishment of the dreams but the aliveness that it gives you today, here in the present. When you are fully alive today, creating with enthusiasm, you are expressing God in you. The word enthusiasm comes from the Greek word, "enthos", which means "with God".

Your dreams are as unique as you are. There is no point in comparing your dreams with others'. My dreams are important to me, but they may not mean anything to you. Your job is to embrace your dream and make a commitment to manifest it in the world.

> *There is a vitality, a life force, an energy, a quickening that is translated through you into action, and because there is only one of you in all of time, this expression is unique. And if you block it, it will never exist through any other medium and it will be lost. The world will not have it. It is not your business to determine how good it is nor how valuable nor how it compares with other expressions. It is your business to keep it yours clearly and directly, to keep the channel open.*

- Martha Graham[11]

If you block the expression of your gifts, the world will never get your contribution. As Martha Graham said, it will never exist through any other medium and will be lost forever.

Your dreams and your life-purpose go hand in hand. Your dreams are a reflection of those things that matter most to you. As you honor your dreams you become clearer with your purpose. As you live your daily life from your purpose, what you dream of accomplishing in the world becomes clearer to you.

---

[11] Martha Graham, quoted by Agnes de Mille. *Martha: The Life and Work of Martha Graham.* Random House, NY (1991).

Manifesting Your Dream In The World

How do we manifest our dreams into reality? Every one of us dreams or has dreamt of accomplishing something in the world. But some have given up on their dreams. Why? The biggest reason people give up on their dreams is that they could not see a way to do it. The gap may be so great between where they are and where they want to be. It does not matter how big this gap may be. **The key is to take baby steps today.** Remember this, all creation takes place in the present. The fulfillment of any dream or project takes time and requires actions that are consistent with your dream. The greatest cathedrals are built brick by brick. This is the same with any thing we create or manifest in the world.

The principles of creation presented in Chapter 5 are the same ones you will need to manifest a dream. Begin by declaring what you are building or creating. Project your mind into the future. What will it look like once completed? Cathedral builders start with a blueprint, a detail of how the building will look once it is completed. It is the same with your dream. Make it as specific as possible and write it down. The result has to be tangible so that you, the creator, will know once the dream has been achieved. The clearer you are with what you intend to produce, the shorter the gap between the time you declared a project and its manifestation in the world. Now ask yourself, what are the steps that I can take now? Break down the project into manageable pieces that can be accomplished in about a month. Treat each step as a project on its own with specific target dates for accomplishment. Put your project down on paper and read it every day until you can speak it without reading it. Do not worry if you cannot see all the steps right now. At this point, it is enough that you see where to begin.

Commitment will transform your dream into reality

Once you are clear what you are creating, **making a commitment** is what will transform your dream into reality. Commitment is a promise that you fully intend to fulfill, like 'no-kidding'. Our relationship with commitment is weak. 'Commit' is a word often used loosely in our culture to mean 'I promise'. We commit to a person or a project and as soon as problems arise, or when a relationship is no longer convenient, we back out. A commitment is a powerful instrument that can keep you in action. This quotation eloquently describes the power of commitments:

> *Commitment is what transforms a promise into reality. It is the words that speak boldly of your intentions and the actions which speak louder than the words. It is making the time when there is none coming through, time after time after time, year after year after year. Commitment is the stuff character is made of; the power to change the face of things.*
>
> *It is the triumph of integrity over skepticism.*

- Author Unknown

A commitment consists of the words that speak your intention, followed by actions that are consistent with that commitment. When you commit, it means you are willing to shut the back door. You are no longer testing whether you like something or not. You are in it for the long haul and you will do what it takes to make a relationship work, or to complete a project.

This is a scary thought for most of us. We do not like to be locked in. We are so used to having options. When we do not like something we purchased, we simply return it and get a refund. Having options is good for some things. The problem is, we relate to almost everything in our life this way. You know what, when it comes to making your dreams a reality, it is not bad to be locked in. In fact, it is a good thing. This is what it takes to make your dream a reality. As soon as you declare your project, life's circumstances will come at you. And if you relate to your dream as anything less than a commitment, watch what happens. There are urgent things to be taken care of, and guess what can wait? Just your dream!

You must be fierce when it comes to fulfilling your dream. When doubts kick in, and you have a thought, "should I do this or not?", just notice it and do it anyway. Consider the steps that you wrote down as promises you make to yourself. And take these promises seriously. Listen, when your child is drowning, you don't stop to think, "should I jump in or not?" You just do! That is the same way you need to be when it comes to taking actions toward your dream. Doubts and hesitancy go away. Sometimes there will be days when you need a break, or you need to step back and get clear what the next step will be. You can make that a part of the process as well. Make a promise that you will give yourself so much time for this step. When you consistently take small steps toward your dream, you can expect miracles. One day you will realize that you have done it.

The above quotation says, "Commitment is the stuff character is made of. It is the triumph of integrity." **You become your word** when your actions are consistent with your promise. This alone – becoming a person of your word – is worth taking the risk of being 'locked in' in a commitment. There is no greater gift you can give yourself than to know that you can rely on your own word.

Commit to take actions today that will move forward your dreams. Countless dreams are killed by procrastination. We wait for the right conditions before we take actions such as, when we have enough money, enough time, or enough talent. Many people think that they have to learn how to do something before they can do it. This is actually the reverse of how learning takes place – we learn by doing. Johann Wolfgang von Goethe (1740-1832) said:

> *Whatever you can do, or dream you can,*
> *begin it.*
> *Boldness has genius, power, and magic*
> *in it.*[12]

I did not know how to write this book before I began. I thought I needed to learn how to write first and quit my job to find time to do it. As long as I thought of the book project this way, it was merely a pipedream - it was never going to happen. Then I made a commitment to write for at least 30 minutes every day. I made time by waking up earlier. Every morning, I showed up in front of

---

[12] Johann W. von Goethe, quoted by Gary W. Fenchuk. *Timeless Wisdom, A Treasury of Universal Truths.* Virginia: Cake Eaters Inc. (2000).

my computer not knowing beforehand what I was going to write about. I took the writing one day, and one step at a time. What I wanted to say became clearer to me each day. Events that were happening in my life became material for this book. People showed up in my life who encouraged me to put this work out in the world when I was tempted to stop. William H. Murray said:

> That the moment one definitely commits oneself, then providence moves too. All sorts of things occur to help one that would never otherwise have occurred.[13]

People who have done great things in the world are not any more talented than you or me. They have simply given themselves permission to start doing what they really wanted to do. Begin doing today what you want to do.

To summarize:

☆ Honoring your dreams and manifesting them in the world lead you to your greatness.

☆ Taking consistent steps towards your dreams gives you aliveness here in the present moment.

☆ Begin by declaring what you want to accomplish.

☆ Set target dates for the accomplishment of the different steps.

---

[13] William H. Murray. *The Scottish Himalayan Expedition.* J.M. Dent & Sons Ltd. (1951).

☆ Make a commitment to take actions consistently to move your project forward.

☆ Do what you want to do today. Begin it and you will learn how to do it.

Questions:

1.) What do you dream of accomplishing? If the answer does not come easy, try these questions as a way to connect you with your dreams:

    a. If you had all the time and money in the world, how would you spend your life?

    b. What is it that you do, that when you are doing it, you forget time and you forget yourself?

    c. What would you do even if you were not paid to do it?

2.) If you find that you are judging your dreams pay attention to that too. What is the thought that comes up for you? When Helen answered that she loves to play music and to kayak, she immediately judged these as irresponsible activities. To be thought of as irresponsible is something that Helen could not be with. Whatever your judgments are about your dreams, remember they are merely thoughts, and they come from fear. Honor your dreams, allow yourself to love what you love, and soon it will become clear how you can make a difference for others through your gifts.

3.) Declare what you are building or creating. What does it look like once it is completed? Imagine how it feels like to have it accomplished.

4.) What steps can you take today that will move forward your dream/project? If there is a big gap between your dream and your current reality, do not get discouraged. The key is to take small actions in strategic places with consistency.

5.) What are the target dates for the steps?

6.) Are there people whom you can include or make requests from to support you in your project?

7.) When will you begin?

Chapter 11

Breakdowns Lead to Breakthroughs

Let us assume that you have now made a commitment to go after your dream. You start taking actions, you're on a roll, and then what happens? Invariably, problems show up. What if a woman who dreams of becoming a medical doctor begins applying to medical schools, and when the responses come back, they are all rejections? She may say, "who am I kidding? I am not fit to be a doctor." What if someone who dreams of writing a book makes a commitment to write every day, and then the children get sick and need her attention? She might say, "I guess it wasn't meant to be." Take heart. Problems or breakdowns are **simply interruptions** to the fulfillment of a commitment, **not** a STOP sign. If you do not have commitments, then anything that happens is acceptable, and there's nothing to be interrupted. This is a path that some people may actually take - we can call it 'going with the flow.' If you do not choose a direction, circumstances and other people will determine it for you. A mentor once said to me, "If you do not have problems, you better start getting suspicious."

Breakdowns provide powerful lessons for our growth. They show us things about ourselves that we would otherwise not see.

Breakdowns reveal what is missing in order to fulfill a commitment or a dream. If you take the stand that you are cause in the matter, breakdowns are instruments for seeing what you are not taking responsibility for. My friend Richard was a research technician with the university. He was doing well in his job and was well liked and appreciated by his boss. But his heart was not in science, it was in music. He had dreams of becoming a musician, of singing and playing his guitar for people. One day he quit his job, joined a band and started singing in pubs and bars. He was ecstatic for about two months until he realized that he was getting deep in debt. The band was not making money and Richard couldn't pay his bills. When we talked about his problem, we saw two things that Richard was not taking responsibility for.

1) First of all, problems with money were not new to him. He was broke even before he joined the band, barely being able to pay his bills from his paycheck. The situation merely amplified his recurring problem. Richard has not taken responsibility for managing his finances.

2) During our conversation, Richard implied that he is not good enough to be a musician. He joined a band whose members did not think highly of themselves. When invited to perform in popular clubs, the bandleader would invite more popular bands to perform with them, and the invited band got paid but their band did not. And the band members just went along with this arrangement. Richard did not take responsibility for having a conversation with the bandleader to say this was not

working and to discuss how things can be changed.

Breakdowns are a gift – they uncover thoughts that hold us back, and our relationship to our projects. **Breakthroughs result from breakdowns.** The dictionary defines "breakthrough" as an event that causes or marks the breaking down of a barrier to progress. You can imagine that the barrier is the wall of the box that you see the world from. When something happens that cannot be solved by what's in the box, it becomes a breakdown. And the only way to solve the problem is to tear down the walls of the box. As such, breakthroughs have far-reaching effects. They change the way you do things to a whole different level. But it takes willingness to look at the situation in another way before a breakthrough can happen. Science has many examples of breakthroughs. In the 1940s, a woman named Barbara McClintock discovered that DNA or genes move around within a cell. This was taken as heresy at that time. Scientists believed that DNA was fixed in place. In short, McClintock's findings did not fit the box. It was not until more than 20 years later, when modern technological tools and instruments were developed that McClintock's discovery was validated. As with any breakthrough, this discovery changed the way we study and think of DNA forever.

Effective people have a powerful relationship with breakdowns. Instead of running from them, they actually anticipate and even create breakdowns. When John F. Kennedy declared in 1961 that we were going to land a man on the moon and bring him back safely before the decade was over, he gave the scientists at NASA a big problem. It was an impossible feat with the technology at that time. On July 20, 1969, U.S. astronauts landed and walked on the moon and returned to earth. Our daily lives today are still impacted by that breakthrough. Our computer and communication technologies would be not be where they are today had it not been for that dream.

Forget The Problem

Once you commit, problems will arise. How do we normally deal with the situation? If we don't quit, we try to solve the problem. Let us say a man and woman in love make a commitment to each other. They get married. Two or three years later, the relationship starts changing, they don't talk anymore like they used to, they have different interests and they spend less time with each other. To salvage the marriage, they have children. The children take up the parents' time, energy, and money. They can't wait until the kids are old enough to leave home. The day comes when the last child leaves home and the couple feel the loneliness of an empty home. They find other solutions to this new problem, and the story goes on. You see, **every solution to a problem today leads to a new problem tomorrow.** Examples are everywhere. Married couples get divorced and find new partners only to find the problems repeating themselves in the form of a new body and face. An unhappy employee finds another job and in a few months he has the same problems.

Here's a possibility – what if we forget about solving the problem (breakdown)? Remember, they are only problems because they are an interruption to your commitment. Instead of solving the problem, go back to your original commitment and reconnect with it.

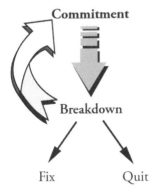

I have observed that when people come to me with problems and I ask them what their commitments are, they often do not know. What happens is that we forget our original intention or commitment, and put our attention on the problems. And what do you think happens when your attention is on the problem? You get more of it.

When you have a breakdown, ask yourself, "What is my commitment here?" Learn from the problem. What is missing in order for you to fulfill that commitment? What are you not taking responsibility for? Maybe it is a thought you have about yourself. Maybe there is a conversation to have with others. Or maybe you said yes when you really meant no, and you have not taken responsibility for your communication. Then ask yourself, "what are other possible ways to fulfill my commitment?"

When I asked Richard what his commitment was, he spoke of using his talents to bring joy to people. He began to see new possibilities to make his dream happen. Richard took a part-time job in a research field that he enjoyed, while he continued performing in the band. He began paying off his debts and learned to manage his finances. Because he was happy, he performed his job well, and he was promoted. Later, Richard realized that he did not have to stick with the same band; that his commitment would be served better if he is part of a band that values the talents of its members. He quit the band and is now looking at the possibility of forming another band. Richard is living his commitment – he is expressing his gifts through his research as well as through music.

The solution we come up with may be only one of the many ways to fulfill our commitment. The problem is, we get attached to that solution and we forget the commitment. When I made a commitment to write this book and started writing for 30 minutes in the morning, there was a point when I began feeling frustrated because I wanted to have more time to write. When I stepped back and asked myself what my commitment was, it became clear that it was about empowering people to express their gifts. I could do this everywhere and anytime in whatever I was doing with people. Even if I did not spend more time writing, the daily events of my life became material for this book and supported my writing. When we step back in the midst of a problem and reconnect with our commitment, new possibilities open up. We begin to see that there is not one fixed way to fulfill our dream.

To summarize:

☆ Problems or breakdowns are simply interruptions to the fulfillment of a commitment.

☆ Breakdowns are powerful instruments for our growth. They uncover what we are not taking responsibility for and what is missing to fulfill our commitment.

☆ Breakdowns lead to breakthroughs. Breakthroughs break down the walls of the box we see the world from and change the way we do things.

☆ Powerful people create breakdowns.

☆ Instead of solving a problem, reconnect with your original commitment. When you are clear what your commitment is, new possibilities will open up.

Questions:

1.) Identify a specific problem that you are in the middle of right now. Write down your answers to the following questions:

   a. What is it an interruption to? In other words, what is your commitment?

b. What is the breakdown telling you about what you are not taking responsibility for?

c. What is missing in order to fulfill your commitment?

d. What are your thoughts that have given rise to this problem? How did those thoughts give rise to the problem?

e. What new declaration will you stand in that is consistent with your commitment?

f. What new possibilities can you see that will move you forward toward your dream?

Chapter 12

The True Joy In Life

In Chapter 9, we asked ourselves, "What am I living for?" And then we asked, "How can I start bringing forth my dreams into the world?" Here is one more question: **Who do you live for?** In your day-to-day activities, who do you serve? Is it your children, or your spouse? Is it your company? Is it your community? Is it your country? Is it God? Or do you live only for yourself? Your answer to this question will determine what you ultimately choose to do with your gifts and dreams.

There's a parable from the Bible that sums up what it takes to choose a life of service for something greater than ourselves. It is called the "Story Of The Talents," extracted from Matthew 25:14-29.

> There was once a man who had three servants. The man was going to go away for an extended period and he entrusted his property to his servants. To one, he gave five talents (a talent here refers to more than a thousand dollars), to another, he gave two talents, and to the third, he gave one talent,

each according to his ability. Then he left. The man who received five talents went at once to put his money to work and gained five more as did the man with two talents. In doing so, each of them doubled their money. But the man who received one talent went off, dug a hole in the ground and hid the money.

After a long time, the master came back and met with his servants. The man who received five talents gave him back ten talents. The man with two talents gave him back four talents. The master was very happy and said to each of them, "Well done! Come share my happiness." When the man with one talent came forward and gave him back the one talent, the master was disappointed. The talent was taken from him and given to the first man with five talents.

Notice that it didn't matter how many talents each of the three men had to begin with. What made the difference was what they chose to do with what they had. Both the man with five talents and the man with two talents doubled what they initially had. But the third man was scared to make a mistake, so he buried his talent. Consequently, his talent did not grow and he ultimately lost it. This is what happens in life too. When we do not use our talents, they eventually atrophy so that no one benefits, including

The True Joy In Life • 107

ourselves. Which one of the three men do you relate to? Does fear stop you from using your talents? Do you ever hide? Fear is natural. It comes with being human. What makes a difference is what we do with that fear.

The other two men (who had five and two talents) were effective – they used their knowledge to increase the money they had. What is the source of the effectiveness of these two men? Their conversations tell us that they had a bigger commitment than to be safe and avoid making mistakes. They both said this, "you entrusted me with talents and I wanted to gain more for you." You can hear the sense of gratitude for having been entrusted with talents. And more importantly, there is a commitment to serve the master. They wanted to gain more for the master. There is a sense of belonging to the master, in contrast to the other man who saw the master as separate from him and who would punish him if he made a mistake.

The master in this story represents something greater than ourselves. I say this is the secret of people who live fulfilling lives. Their life is not about them. **It is about something greater than they are.** They feel they are part of a larger whole, whether it is a community, the world, or God. Serving that greater whole is their reason for living.

George Bernard Shaw (1856-1950) said this:

> *This is the true joy in life, being used*
> *for a purpose recognized by yourself as*
> *a mighty one; the being a force of nature*
> *instead of a feverish, selfish little clod of*

> *ailments and grievances complaining that*
> *the world will not devote itself to making*
> *you happy.*

George Bernard Shaw saw that when our attention is on our-selves and what we want, life becomes a suffering. We complain and blame others when the world is not giving us what we want. He further said:

> *I am of the opinion that my life belongs to the*
> *whole community and as long as I live, it is*
> *my privilege to do for it whatever I can.*

George Bernard Shaw was one of the most prolific writers of his time. He did not spend his time worrying how good his work was, and what others thought of him. He was bold and he told the truth. And he lived by his word, "It is a privilege to serve."

Coming from the stand that what we do with our life impacts others can empower us during difficult times, when nothing seems to be working and we just want to give up on our dreams. The story of a scientist named Buckminster Fuller is an example. At age 32, Buckminster Fuller was ready to kill himself. His first child had just died. He was bankrupt, discredited, had a wife and a new-born daughter. In despair, feeling like a complete failure, he did not know how he was going to take care of his family. Just as he was about to jump from the bridge to the freezing waters of Lake Michigan he had an epiphany.[14] It was as if he heard a voice that said, "Your life does not belong to you. It belongs to the universe."

---

[14] The Buckminster Fuller Institute. http://www.bfi.org/introduction_to_bmf.htm

He stopped and sobbed, vowing to make his life count from that moment. He embarked on an "experiment to discover what the little penniless, unknown individual might be able to do effectively on behalf of humanity"[15]. Buckminster Fuller became one of the century's greatest inventors. He was also a philosopher, a poet and a humanist. He was most known for his invention of the geodesic dome, a structure shaped like a piece of a sphere or a ball, which is amazingly strong and cost-effective. There are about 300,000 geodesic domes today. Some of these provide cheap shelters to families in Africa at a cost of $350 per dome. Fuller spent his life developing architectural designs that attempt to anticipate and solve humanity's major problems through the highest technology by providing "more and more life support for everybody with less and less resources." What a loss to the world if Fuller had taken his life!

This is what he had to say about the role of each individual:

> *You do not have the right to eliminate yourself, you do not belong to you. You belong to the universe. The significance of you will forever remain obscure to you, but you may assume that you are fulfilling your significance if you apply yourself to converting all your experience to the highest advantage of others. You and all men are here for the sake of other men.*[16]

---

[15] Buckminster Fuller and Anwar Dil. *Humans in Universe.* New York: Mouton (1983).

[16] Buckminster Fuller. *Ideas and Integrities.* Edited by Robert W. Marks. New Jersey: Prentice-Hall (1963).

Fuller saw that we are all interconnected and we are all stewards of "spaceship earth." Our eyes tell us that we are separate from other human beings. That we live in a country that is separate from other countries. That people are divided into races based on color. We forget that these are all artificial divisions made by man. From a distance, when astronauts are in space and look down on earth, they see one ball, united, not divided into parts. That ball we call earth contains all the problems of humanity - wars, famines, poverty — as well as all the victory and glory of human history. Seen from afar, humankind is one and interconnected.

It does not matter what your social standing may be, how high or low you think it is. Your life matters! What you do with your gifts impacts not just you, but the world. You are unique. There will never be another one that will have the same combination of experiences and gifts as you.

George Bernard Shaw further said:

> *I want to be thoroughly used up when I*
> *die, for the harder I work, the more I live...*
> *Life is not a "brief candle" to me. It is a sort*
> *of splendid torch, which I have got hold of*
> *for the moment, and I want to make it burn*
> *as brightly as possible before handing it on*
> *to future generations.*

Do not let the torch that has been given to you die with you. Your gifts are for the world. As Ralph Waldo Emerson (1803-82) said, "to know that even one life has breathed easier because you have lived", is to have succeeded in life.[17]

Live each moment as if it were your last. Give it your all.

To summarize:

⭐ We are not separate from other people and what we do with our life and gifts impacts others.

⭐ Living a meaningful life is a function of what and who we live for.

⭐ When we live the possibility that we are part of a community or humanity, our relationship with our commitments becomes more powerful. It grants a sense of accountability that is beyond just ourselves. Our lives become more than "it is all about me."

Questions:

1.) Coming from the point of view that we are not separate, who are the people that will miss out the most if you do not express your gifts? In other words, who are the people that you want to impact the most?

2.) Write your eulogy from the point of view of those people that you want to have impacted in your life. What do you want them to say? How have you impacted their lives? What will live

---

[17] Ralph Waldo Emerson, quoted by Gary W. Fenchuk. *Timeless Wisdom, A Treasury of Universal Truths*. Virginia:Cake Eaters Inc. (2000).

on in them because you have lived?

3.) Will those people be able to say these things about you today if you died unexpectedly? If you answered no, are you willing to start living for a higher purpose now?

Part III

Summary

Our journey together has taken us from an awareness of our thoughts that shape our behavior and actions, to choosing empowering thoughts that allow the expression of our greatest possibilities, and finally to living our lives for a purpose greater than our own selves. Empowering choices become clear when we know what matters to us. When we allow ourselves to love what we love, it will lead us to our greatness. That is why honoring our dreams is so important. At some point, we want to leave a lasting legacy in the world. When you know you are part of the human community, then you know that your life matters. What you do or don't do with your gifts impacts the world.

In a real sense all life is interrelated. All men are caught in an inescapable network of mutuality, tied in a single garment of destiny. Whatever affects one directly affects all indirectly. I can never be what I ought to be until you are what you ought to be, and you can never be what you ought to be until I am what I ought to be. This is the interrelated structure of reality.

- Martin Luther King Jr.

OWN YOUR GREATNESS

Epilogue

It is from our thoughts that everything we create emanates and we have the power to choose our thoughts. Owning our greatness is as simple as bringing ourselves to the present, becoming aware of our thoughts, and choosing thoughts that are in alignment with our invented purpose.

Greatness is not a destination. It is a way of being. It is being clear about our deepest commitments - what and who we are living for. And then thinking, speaking, and acting in ways that are consistent with those commitments. Greatness is not about doing extraordinary things, or being extraordinarily gifted. It is about doing ordinary things with extraordinary love.

To own our greatness is to own our humanity, as well as our magnificence. It is a life-long, continuous process and is never a done-deal. This process is like peeling an onion. All that we need to be great is already here. Our job is to keep peeling the layers (thoughts) that mask the greatness that is our essence. When you get to the core, all there is, is love. When you come from love, you are living your greatness.

> *Finally, remember that the present is all we have. Live each day from love and the possibility that you make a difference. You do!*

Dear Reader:

Acknowledge yourself for completing this book. It is a statement of your commitment to your own development. Remember that personal growth is a life-long process. We don't figure it out and then our life is fixed forever. We will still have our habitual thoughts, but we are not at their effect whenever we are aware of them being there. The thoughts are just there and they can co-exist with an empowering thought that we choose to stay with in the present moment.

When you feel like quitting when the same old problems come up, do not lose heart. Life has its high and low points. If you continue practicing awareness of your thoughts and choosing ones that empower you, over time, your low points in life will be at a higher point than what you have considered to be your high points before.

Life is all about growing into who we really are. Enjoy the journey.

God bless you.

Sincerely,
Nora Lapitan

Index

OWN YOUR GREATNESS
A Guide to Creating a Life with
Boundless Possibilities

ORDER FORM

Postal Orders: Empowered Living LLC, 1020 Braidwood Ct.,
Fort Collins, CO 80524-9694   Telephone: (970) 217-1193

FAX Orders: (970) 407-9981. Send this form.

E-Mail Orders: orders@Own-Your-Greatness.com

Qty	Unit Price	Title		TOTAL
		Own Your Greatness		
			Subtotal	
			Sales Tax (CO add 6.5%)	
			TOTAL	

Payment enclosed: ❑ Check   ❑ Money Order

Payable to: Empowered Living LLC

Please charge my: ❑ Visa   ❑ Mastercard   ❑ American Express   ❑ Discover

Credit Card No: _____ Exp Date: _____

Signature on Card: _____

Name on Card: _____

Address: _____

City: _____ State: _____ Zip:_____

Phone no. in case we need to call you regarding your order _____

Enclose $4.00 for priority mail for one book (plus $1.00 for additional book).

Canadian and foreign orders payable in US funds. Canadian and Mexican orders add
$2.00 postage. Other foreign orders enclose $7.50 postage. Your orders will be shipped
surface rate unless special shipping fee arrangements are made.

OWN YOUR GREATNESS
A Guide to Creating a Life with
Boundless Possibilities

ORDER FORM

Postal Orders: Empowered Living LLC, 1020 Braidwood Ct.,
Fort Collins, CO 80524-9694   Telephone: (970) 217-1193

FAX Orders: (970) 407-9981. Send this form.

E-Mail Orders: orders@Own-Your-Greatness.com

Qty	Unit Price	Title		TOTAL
		Own Your Greatness		
			Subtotal	
			Sales Tax (CO add 6.5%)	
			TOTAL	

Payment enclosed: ❏ Check   ❏ Money Order

Payable to: Empowered Living LLC

Please charge my: ❏ Visa   ❏ Mastercard   ❏ American Express   ❏ Discover

Credit Card No: _____ Exp Date: _____

Signature on Card: _____

Name on Card: _____

Address: _____

City: _____ State: _____ Zip:_____

Phone no. in case we need to call you regarding your order _____

Enclose $4.00 for priority mail for one book (plus $1.00 for additional book).

Canadian and foreign orders payable in US funds. Canadian and Mexican orders add $2.00 postage. Other foreign orders enclose $7.50 postage. Your orders will be shipped surface rate unless special shipping fee arrangements are made.